Praise for a Reason to Live

After reading the first chapter of this book, it touched me so
deeply that I reconsidered my thoughts of suicide.
—A High School Student who has since found significant recovery

This is a story that needs to be told. It will comfort countless
mothers whose children suffer from addiction.
—Leila Russell, a mother who lost her son to a drug overdose

This deep and pervasive book moved me to tears. I felt sad,
strong, and elated. I felt the energy behind Beverly's acts when
she considered herself less than 100% or 0%. With transparency,
she bore her heart to the world as her son altered the course of
countless lives. Beverly's ability to love and find light in every soul is
crushing! Her descriptive flow and tone wove images in my mind.
—Thomas S., Health Care Worker

This is one book that I couldn't put down!
It deepens my sympathy for troubled persons who
self-medicate with illegal drugs.
—Elizabeth Mercado, mother of a recovered meth addict

Other Books by Beverly Ann Needham

If You Are Struggling—
One Woman's Journey Through Bipolar Disorder,
Trauma, and a Split Personality

To Be Released soon:

Twenty-Six Miles
by Beverly Ann Needham

Twenty-Six Miles is a true story about a woman who faces graffiti on her living room walls, testifies in court against a serial rapist and murderer, and deals with loss, a split personality, marriage to a rocket scientist, and her own Irish temper. She ran her first marathon while fighting her second brain tumor. Subsequent marathons have calmed her temper and saved her marriage and health. In the marathon of life, he who runs with the most love wins.

A Reason
to Live

Beverly Ann Needham

To order additional copies of this book, contact:
Bookwhip
1-855-339-3589
www.bookwhip.com

Significant Persons in this Book

Parents:

Gregory A. Needham - born 1952
Beverly Ann Needham - born 1953

Children:

Tim - born 1977
Jeff - born 1977 - 8 minutes after his twin brother
Eli - born 1979
Christy - born 1980
Butterfly - born 1982
Phillip - born 1984
Matthew (Matt) - born 1992
James- Born 1992 - Matthew's friend who we raised as one of our own

Some names in this book are pseudonyms.

No One Can Take Your Place

You may think
That the world does not need you,
But it does.

For you are unique, like no one
That has ever come before,
Or will come after.

No one can speak with your voice,
Say your piece, smile your smile, or shine your light.
No one can take your place,
For it is yours alone to fill.

If you are not there to shine your light,
Who knows how many travelers will lose their way
As they try to pass by your empty place in the darkness.

(A quote by Julia M. Landis, inspired by a poem
found in Massachusetts's Kripalu Center)

PROLOGUE

Christmas Day 2006
Simi Valley, California

Greg and I drove to the Wal-Mart parking lot to pick up our son Jeff. Jeff is one of many homeless people in our town. He's proud of himself for making it on his own, in his own way. Yet Jeff wouldn't miss Christmas dinner at Grandma Fawn's House. No. Many a year he has worked hard to sober up for a night with his relatives, where he sits back in a chair with his long legs stretched out, and a relaxed look on his face.

We drove up to the front of the store and saw Jeff, yet he didn't look our way. He was staring at a man with tattooed biceps bulging out of his tank top. This burly man—who stood a few yards from Jeff—had a brick in his hand, which he was preparing to throw at our son. There was already a brick lying at Jeff's feet which he had apparently dodged.

"Jeff, get in the car! Let's go!" I urged when we pulled in front of the store.

Jeff wouldn't budge—his eyes fixed on the bully.

"Get in the car! We've got to go to Grandma's house NOW!" I shouted.

The man tensed up, pulled back his arm and aimed, ready to throw the brick.

I lunged out of the car, ran between the two of them and began singing, "The first Noel the angels did say, was to certain poor shepherds in fields as they lay..." The bully lowered his brick and stared at me like I was crazy. I even got the attention of Jeff, took him by the hand, and led him to our van.

We began driving out of the Wal-Mart parking lot and smelled alcohol on Jeff's breath. The "No Alcohol" rule at Grandma's house requires Jeff not come inside unless he's sober. *Maybe we can eat Christmas dinner outside,* I mused.

Suddenly, Jeff cried out, "That guy threw a brick at me for no reason!"

Jeff swung his fist and crushed the side window of our van. Greg pulled over as Jeff pulled his arm back in the van, and glass fell on the ground.

Jeff wasn't cut, but tears filled his eyes. Ashamed, he slowly opened the van door, stepped out, and walked back toward the hills where he lived in a tent.

Greg and I stepped out of the car, held onto each other for comfort, and watched Jeff walk toward the woods. As he disappeared beyond the trees, I felt glass grinding under my shoes. *Is this the fifteenth or sixteenth window Jeff has broken? I've lost count.*

PART ONE

CHAPTER ONE

In February of 2010, my editors Danielle and Karrilynn came to my office to discuss my latest book, "Healing the Heart." Danielle held up my manuscript, saying, "This book is not coming together. However, every time you write about Jeff, your writing is at its best. You should pull together everything you've ever written about Jeff and put it into one book."

"Yes!" exclaimed Karrilynn. "You should write a book about what you're going through. It will help a lot of mothers who are going through the same thing."

"No way!" I argued. "I could never write a book about Jeff!"

I shook my head and remembered the last time I saw him.

Jeff had called me from the hills where he lived.

"I borrowed someone's cell phone," he said. "I thought you might like to take me shopping."

"Have you been drinking?" I asked.

"No," he replied, sounding proud of himself.

I drove to the hills and parked my van. I saw him walking down the hillside. He had no shirt, was wearing only shorts, and was barefoot on a cold winter day. *There's no way he can be sober,* I said to myself. *He always takes his shirt and shoes off when he's on Crystal Meth.*

I locked the van door and waited on the path. When he stood before me I was appalled by the sight of snot hanging from his nose like a snake. "I thought you said you were sober."

Jeff replied, "You asked if I was drinking. You didn't ask if I was on drugs."

I took off my jacket to hand it to him. "It's cold. Take this," I said.

Jeff folded his arms across his bare chest, refusing to take my jacket. "I'm fine," he said.

I tried not to look at the snot running down his beard, but it nauseated me. I went to my van to get some paper towels.

A memory flashed through my mind of a much younger Jeff with a constantly dripping nose. I wiped his nose more than the noses of all six of my other children combined. But Jeff was a man now. Six feet and seven inches tall.

I offered him paper towels, saying, "Here's something to wipe your nose with."

"I don't want to wipe my nose. It will just run again," he replied.

I turned to leave, saying, "I can't take you shopping when you're not sober. Goodbye."

Jeff watched me walk to my van and get inside. I called out, "Call me when you're sober." Then I drove away, rounded a corner, and began to cry.

"No, I could never write a book about Jeff," I said.

"Please think about it," Danielle and Karrilynn urged.

"No," I said. "It would be too hard." I had no intention of giving it another thought.

A few nights later, at midnight, Greg and I were asleep when I felt an electric shock jolt through me. Alarmed and confused, I looked at Greg to see if he had felt it. He was sound asleep. Yet I was electrified with energy that filled every part of me. A power came over me—a burning desire to write a book about Jeff.

I turned on my lamp. Greg turned over and pulled the sheet over his eyes. I gently kissed him, grateful that I can write in the middle of the night without complaint from him. Then I picked up my pen and began outlining the chapters. *Jeff's life is full already. Completing his story will be easy*, I thought. Gently, yet powerfully, the title for the book came into my mind: *A Reason to Live.*

Seven hours later, sunlight streamed through my window and danced on my finished draft of Jeff's life from his birth until his present age of 32 years. I glanced at the clock and dashed to my closet to get ready for choir rehearsal. I grabbed my stack of music and tried to review the songs. As choir director, I needed to be ready. Yet, all I could think about was, *I'm writing a book about Jeff!* Greg woke up and with interest listened to me tell him about the book.

At church, I welcomed a new girl to choir rehearsal. I gave her a hug and placed her between my sweetest singers. They smiled at her. I wished people would have welcomed Jeff when he was her age.

Down the hall from where the choir was rehearsing, a younger Jeff once jumped on top of his chair and yelled profanities in his Sunday School class. Before the teacher arrived, one of the students told him, "We Don't Want You Here!" Back then, I found Jeff wandering the hallway alone.

Although I couldn't rewrite Jeff's childhood, I felt happy to see the new girl fit in.

After church, 17-year-old Matthew poked his head into my room. "Mom, we're playing a game of Catch Phrase. Will you join us?"

Matt stood in my doorway, patiently waiting for my answer. Born during the darkest years of my life, Matt kept me alive—because he needed me.

I marveled that he, our seventh and last child, was now playing High School Basketball and working as a cadet with the fire department.

Matt and I walked into the living room and Greg smiled. After all these years he still melts my heart with his baby face and his innocent smile. He resembles Paul McCartney of the Beatles. Yet he's a world-renowned rocket scientist who has worked on the space shuttle engine and the Hubble telescope.

Jeff's twin brother Tim sat beside his wife Brandy holding their newborn son Orion. Tim's family rented part of our house.

Matt took a seat by James, his childhood friend. We had taken James in as one of our own a few years earlier. James' father had knocked on our door, saying, "We've been evicted from our home and have nowhere to sleep except in my truck. Can James spend the night with Matt?" James has lived with us ever since, sharing his music, cooking, and love.

Our game of Catch Phrase played out—the girls against the boys. We were tied and it was my turn to give a clue. I plucked an ivy leaf from a house plant and called out, "Yale! Harvard! Columbia! Princeton!" The timer had but one second left when Brandy shouted, "Ivy League!" We were cheering when a knock sounded on our front door and in walked our daughter Christy with her husband Steve.

"We're hiking up Hummingbird Trail. Does anybody want to come?" Christy asked.

I grabbed my camera while Matt got our dogs. Then all of us piled into cars and drove to the east hills of Simi Valley. Simi, formerly home to an Indian tribe, was named after their word Shimiyi, meaning *little wind cloud*. A breeze wafted through the rock canyon as our dogs, Jonny and Jasmine splashed in a stream. I reflected on how Jonny and Jasmine joined our family.

Jonny was a dingo pup I had rescued five years earlier while living in Utah with Jeff, during Jeff's last recovery from drug abuse.

Jasmine was a shepherd pup that Tim found wandering alone on a railroad track. Tim was into drugs and alcohol at the time. Yet he came to our home holding Jasmine in his arms and asked, "Can I move home? If I can keep this pup, I won't drink." I started to say No, because Tim's former dog had chewed up the couch and the carpet. Yet I'd been praying for Tim to not get killed driving drunk through the hills on his motorcycle. *Is Jasmine an answer to my prayers?* I wondered. That night, Jasmine slept in Tim's arms, replacing the beer bottle, and Tim began his recovery. That was years ago.

The dogs finished drinking from the stream. We began our climb up Hummingbird Trail. I thought of Jeff camping in the west hills of Simi. I hoped he was enjoying the sunshine and fresh air like I was.

From the mountain top we viewed the ocean. The sun dipped below the horizon as we began our descent.

Back at home, Greg and the rest of our family enjoyed root beer floats. I went to bed. With my head on my pillow I scanned through the pictures I took of our hike. The last image I saw before dozing off was a picture of Christy standing on a ledge, smiling at me at sunset. Although exhausted, I wouldn't have given up this day for anything.

I'd barely fallen asleep when my phone rang. I answered, murmuring a hello.

"Hi, I'm calling from Freedom House. We might have an opening for Jeff tomorrow. Can you find him and sober him up? He needs to pass the drug test before we'll take him back."

Ten years earlier, Jeff got his first DUI. He was court ordered to attend Freedom House. Back then Jeff did well. The director even hoped Jeff would stay on as staff. With this second court order I hoped Jeff would heal from his addictions for good. Yet he kept walking out of the sober house.

How will I find Jeff to take him back to Freedom House? I wondered. I remembered Jeff saying, "Don't go in the hills looking for me. It's not safe."

I prayed for help, and Jeff's friend Bridget came to mind. Bridget lived under a bridge near egrets, ducks, and sometimes thousands of baby frogs. I called her cell phone and asked where Jeff was.

"I saw him walking toward the AM/PM market. You can probably catch him there," she said.

Sprinkles of rain fell as I parked in the AM/PM parking lot. I walked inside and saw a long line of customers. "Have you seen a 6 ½ foot tall man, with a long blond ponytail?" I asked the cashier.

"No," the cashier replied, sounding annoyed. I felt alone, although I was surrounded by people. Then I noticed a woman standing behind me, looking at me. I sensed she knew that I was the mother of the lost man I had described and that she understood how I felt. Our eyes locked and she said, "Good luck."

With renewed hope, I walked out of the market, got back in my van, and drove toward the homeless camps. Then, suddenly I remembered that there was a liquor store nearby. I turned toward the store and passed a man in tattered clothes, walking with his head hanging down. I assumed he was an elderly stranger. After passing him, I looked back through my rearview mirror and saw that the gingerly walking man was barefoot. To my surprise, I realized it was Jeff. I stopped the van and waited for him. He lifted his head, happy to see me.

"I'm glad I found you," I said. "Can I take you to our boat so you can get ready to go back into Freedom House?"

Jeff sat on the front seat, cold and shivering. He said not a word.

"I'll drive home to get some supplies. Then, can I take you to our boat?" I asked again.

Jeff nodded. I threw him a blanket from the back seat, and drove home, thankful that I had been able to find him.

I parked across the street from our home—the house that Jeff had grown up in. "You stay here," I said. Because of all the windows Jeff had broken in our home, a restraining order was in effect, to keep him from coming within fifty feet of our house. I crossed the street to enter our house and looked for something for Jeff to eat.

Shortly after, I returned to Jeff with fish tacos—compliments of James who was fixing his dinner, and hard boiled eggs—compliments of Matthew who was fixing his school lunch for the next day. Jeff began to eat, and I returned to our house for supplies to take to the harbor where our boat was docked. Greg watched me pack, knowing that when I have my mind made up to do something, there is little he can do to stop me.

As I took the box of food and my dog out the door Greg asked, "Is Jeff sober?" I didn't reply. Greg was worried, yet I focused on taking Jeff to our boat, not on comforting Greg.

Jeff's twin, Tim said, "Mom, don't go. You've helped Jeff enough." He was thinking of Jeff's ex-girlfriend who had stabbed her mother to death. Yet I ignored his caution.

"Goodbye. I love you," I said as I gave Greg a hug, and walked away.

Tim stepped onto the porch. "We love you too. Be safe," he said.

I started the van's engine for our 45-mile drive to the harbor and Jeff spoke. "Can I bring Beta?" he asked.

There flashed through my mind the memory of when I first saw Beta: *Jeff had walked out of Freedom House, and later called from a pay phone. He mumbled and stuttered, "Ahh, ahh, ahh, c-c-can you go to the boat? I, I,*

I'm worried about my fish and my crab. I left them on the boat. Wait! No! I remember now! I slept with the crab. When I woke up the crab was- ahh, he was- ahh- He was gone! No! Now I remember. It crawled under some papers. No! Wait. Now I remember—I, I sold it. But I'm worried about my fish. Will you check on it?"

I went to the harbor after this conversation, imagining a dead fish inside the boat's cabin. I stepped below deck, holding my nose. There I found a small fish bowl with a purple Japanese fighting fish, a Beta with long delicate fins, swimming around in circles. I took Beta home.

I smiled at the memory and went back inside to get Beta, gently carrying his bowl to the car. Jeff held the fishbowl on his lap as we drove. Jeff's never in a hurry. Like me, he's happy to take the rural route rather than the freeway. I stopped to take a picture of the moon glowing through a break in the trees. Jeff didn't mind me stopping. With Jeff, time stands still.

We arrived at Channel Islands Harbor where our sailboat floated quietly in its slip. From between the clouds, the moon's reflection danced on the water.

CHAPTER TWO

I remember the first time that Jeff and Tim asked for a boat. They were three-years-old. I promised them that we'd buy a boat after we paid off the second loan on our home. I thought Greg was in sync with my promise so the twins and I spent little of his paycheck for luxuries.

We made homemade gluten from scratch to use as a meat substitute. We also made granola, graham crackers, and homemade cheese. We ground wheat kernels into flour and used the flour to make bread. I kneaded the bread dough with the help of eight tiny hands—the hands of the twins, their little brother Eli, and their baby sister Christy. They wore cloth diapers which I hung on our clothesline to dry as the boys rode tricycles beneath the white fabric billowing like sails. I hadn't considered that our dream of buying a boat wouldn't come true. Yet, after we paid the second loan on our home, Greg had no interest. He felt uncomfortable with us buying a boat. In silent resentment, I failed to work out the important matter at that time.

However, Jeff never forgot my promise. He relentlessly looked at boat ads for nearly thirty years.

When Jeff and I finally started looking at boats together, he found a 70 foot sailboat and begged me to buy it. I was frightened of the monstrous thing. It looked like a pirate ship, with enormous colorful sails and more ropes holding the sails up than I could count. We hadn't even learned how to sail yet and I said, No.

Later, Greg took me to look at another sailboat. Captain Sean Quine—the owner of the boat—offered to give me sailing lessons as part of the sale. We bought his Hunter racing sailboat, a 25½ foot white boat with gold trim. Below deck were clean couches, beds and kitchen space which won my heart. Even Greg thought it was a nice boat. I finally kept my promise and named our boat Dream Reviver. Yet, Jeff was not around. He had landed in jail for drug possession.

Initially, I learned to sail quicker than any other student Captain Quine had. I learned so fast that he took me on the open sea for my first lesson—which he had never done before with a new student.

When Jeff got out of jail, we slated a sailing lesson for Jeff and his twin Tim.

Later, Tim took Jeff on a weekend sailing trip to Anacapa Island. Jeff was drunk most of the way, but Tim was patient. Their only mishap was a cabin fire that started on the boat's stove. As the flames shot up, Tim thought, *If the boat goes down, at least we'll be rescued—there are other boats nearby.* Yet the boys found the fire extinguisher and put the fire out.

In time, Greg, Tim, and Jeff became such good sailors that I forgot how to sail. I'd sit with my feet dangling over the bow and watch for dolphins while the men did all the work.

Some people say that having a boat is like having a bottomless pit to throw money into. But to me, having a boat is having a heart full of dreams.

I remembered the emotional day we spent on our boat together last Thanksgiving 2009.

Jeff had been waiting to get back into Freedom House after walking out. On Thanksgiving Day, I picked him up from a corner where he panhandled, and took him to our boat. There, I settled in the boat's cabin to rest, while Jeff stretched out on deck, using life vests to cushion his long body. That Thanksgiving Day the harbor was quiet.

My phone rang and my son-in-law Steve said, "We will miss you at Thanksgiving dinner."

Steve had only been a part of our family for a year, and already he shared our grief over having a missing person. I loved watching Steve play basketball with Matthew and chum around with my other children. Yet, sadly, Steve did not even know Jeff.

"It's nice that you're staying with Jeff so he won't have to spend Thanksgiving alone," Steve said. "It shows how much you care about each of your children."

After Steve's phone call, the boat rocked as Jeff opened the door to the cabin and plopped down beside me. "There was a rattlesnake in the hills, as thick as my neck," Jeff said. "Some people wanted to kill it. But I wouldn't let them. It wasn't hurting anybody." Then Jeff looked down and whispered, "When I was gone, someone killed it." He began to cry, "I didn't want them to kill it. I kept watching it and kept people away from it. But then, while I was gone, they killed it."

I thought of the love Jeff had for all living creatures, ever since he was a child. When he played with his cars on the windowsill, he collected flies that had gotten inside the house. He took off their wings so they'd fit in his cars. Later he sadly asked, "Why did the flies die after I put them in my cars?"

Now, Jeff at 6 ½ feet tall, still had a tender heart. Jeff broke the silence, saying, "I got it— I got it from—," he stammered without finishing.

"What did you get?" I asked.

He continued as if he didn't hear me, saying, "I wanted to see what it would feel like to shoot myself in the foot."

I stared at Jeff, not knowing he had a gun. Then he began to cry. His chest heaved out with every sob. Then, as suddenly as he had started crying, he stopped, and laughed, saying, "I decided not to shoot my foot! I decided to shoot my leg instead. But when I pulled the trigger the gun didn't go off! It didn't go off!!" he repeated as if it was some kind of joke.

I felt paralyzed by the painful truth: If nothing changed, my son would kill himself—if not by an overdose, then by a senseless act. I thought of the hills where he lived and pictured him lying somewhere in the woods, bleeding from a gunshot wound and unable to walk for help. I wanted to tell Jeff how much I loved him. I wanted him to live! Yet no words could get past the lump in my throat.

Jeff silently stared into space. Then he spoke again, "Some people started fighting and it got bad." He began to cry.

I wanted to put my arms around him and comfort him. Yet, ever since he was a small child he hasn't liked being touched except on rare occasions. Jeff cried himself to sleep, and I walked to the seashore. I sat down on the sand. Watching the sparkling waves calmed me. A feeling of love washed over me. I knew that I could face whatever lay ahead with Jeff. I returned to the boat and found Jeff sitting on the dock, intoxicated. I felt so much peace at that moment that seeing him drunk could not diminish my love for him.

The next day, Jeff announced, "I can't drink today because I want to go to Grandma's house. I want to see my family." That night with happy anticipation, Jeff was ready to go to Grandma's Post Thanksgiving Feast.

After Thanksgiving, I ignored weather forecasts of heavy snows and took Jeff to Southern Utah when Freedom House still had no opening. The roads were covered with snow when we arrived in the small town of Orderville. All was still, except for the snow that kept falling all night. Traffic stopped.

The power went out and the hum of electrical appliances became silent. I've never heard anything like it. It was the biggest silence I've ever heard. After a long search, Jeff found a candle in the back of a cupboard and gave it to me so I could read and write.

A few days later, Jeff shoveled several feet of snow away from our car and we returned to California. He was admitted back into Freedom House, not far from our family boat.

That December, Jeff stayed on our boat with me again. He had walked out of Freedom House, but wanted to get back in. We went to a church by the harbor where they served a Mexican potluck dinner. Jeff ignored warnings to take only a drop of something they called "Death Salsa." Jeff knew no one who could handle hot peppers like he could. So he gulped down a large portion, followed by more water than I'd ever seen him drink.

After dinner, we drove up the Pacific Coast Highway while the fire in his gut subsided. It was four days until Christmas and Jeff was not allowed to visit our home because of the restraining order. I missed Greg badly. Even the sight of the waves splashing water onto the highway didn't lift the homesickness welling up in my chest. Yet I remembered something a person said at church, "I look for needy people to help at Christmas time." At that moment, we passed two transients.

"Let's see if they'd like a ride," I said.

"We passed them already," Jeff replied, adding, "We can pick them up on our way back." Then, within a mile Jeff said, "Let's turn back."

We turned back and pulled over. One man was pushing a rundown bicycle while walking with a limp. The other man was walking with his dog to his grandma's house—over 100 miles away. They were relieved to get in our van with us. Their names were Phil and Matt—the names of my two youngest sons. My loneliness was forgotten.

I obliged when Phil made a request, "I once had a free dinner at the Oxnard Rescue Mission. Do you think we can eat there?"

"Certainly," I replied, turning in the direction of the mission.

"You're going the wrong way," Jeff told me. But I didn't listen, anxious to take what I thought was a short cut. Jeff sat calmly while I drove further and further into unfamiliar territory. Finally, I admitted I was lost. Jeff quickly showed me the way to the mission, barely in time for dinner.

After eating, I asked Jeff if we could invite Phil and Matt to spend the night on our boat. Jeff agreed.

I chuckle as I remember Matt gingerly stepping aboard. With caution he watched his dog, and asked if there was any chance his dog would get seasick. I didn't tell Matt how funny his question was, but laughed to myself as I answered, "No, at the dock, the boat doesn't toss enough to make you sick."

Our guests settled in. "Two nights ago," Phil said, "I slept on a park bench by the sea, wondering what it would be like to sleep on a boat. Now, I've got my wish."

The next morning, Jeff and I drove the transients to their destination in Santa Barbara and listened to them "oooh" and "aaah" over the sights, not being used to traveling inside a car.

Then, Jeff and I got a tree, decorations, clothes and hot chocolate for a poor family that we had heard about at church. It was a family with lots of children. The dad was crippled, and the mom was battling cancer.

Later, Jeff and I slept in our boat while it heaved back and forth in a storm. The wind howled and the boat groaned. Yet, I loved being there with Jeff. I smiled at the memory of him not getting stressed when I got lost on the way to the mission for dinner. Other people might make fun of me for getting lost—or disapprove of me picking up transients. Most of my family makes fun of me for driving such an old van. Yet with Jeff, none of these things matter. It was almost worth it to get lost—just to see how patient Jeff would be with me. Jeff, the one who is not allowed on our property, sometimes is the gentlest of all—when his mind is not altered by drugs.

The day before Christmas, Jeff and I went sailing fast and far in a strong wind, and with huge swells. We sailed to the oil rigs where dozens of seals barked "Hello" to us. We barked back and wished them a Merry Christmas. Then we saw a huge sea lion on a buoy. He puffed out his chest and threatened a deep-voiced warning, marking his territory. We barked back.

That night, we were depressed over saying goodbye as Jeff walked back into Freedom House when they finally had an opening. After he left, I walked around the block with my dog Jonny, wiping tears from my eyes.

I slept in my van on E Street that night, next to the Catholic Church and around the corner from Freedom House, too tired to drive home.

My Son Jeff
People say he's socially different
Yet he takes time to talk to people whom others ignore.
People say he's slow
Yet when everyone else is busy he has time to help a stranger.
They said he couldn't concentrate on the schoolwork
Yet he can fix things that nobody else can fix.

On Christmas Day, Jeff was allowed to leave Freedom House for a few hours. We set out to sea. The water was still, like glass. Only a slight breeze. Jeff took over the sails and the rudder with ease as we sailed toward Malibu.

On the way, we came to a 1,000 foot cliff called Mugu Rock. The magnificent protruding rock beside the Pacific Coast Highway can be seen for miles. Yet from down below, in the sea, it looked entirely different. Peaceful. Majestic. On the quiet sea beneath the massive rock, in our little boat, it felt as if we were on another planet.

Our quiet repose ended when Jeff changed the direction of the sails to head back to the harbor. The breeze stopped. We lost momentum. After waiting, Jeff turned on the motor and we made it back to the harbor in 30 minutes—covering the same area which had taken three hours to sail through earlier.

After the holidays, I returned to our boat to recover from exhaustion. The stress of the holidays and of helping Jeff, had taken its toll. I planned to spend a few days alone at the harbor while Jeff remained in Freedom House.

It was quiet and dark when I arrived at the harbor. No ripple on the water. Not even the sound of a creaking boat could be heard. I walked down the ramp onto the dock and stopped. There was a light on inside our boat.

Who would sneak into our boat? I wondered.

I walked away from the boat and called harbor patrol. "I came to spend the night on my boat," I said. "But someone's in it and I don't know who it is. I'm afraid to go inside. Could you send somebody over?"

While I waited, I discounted my suspicion. *No. It couldn't be Jeff. I had just helped him get back into Freedom House on Christmas Eve.*

The harbor patrolwoman pulled up in her boat. I feared more that my suspicion was right, than that a stranger was on board. "I came to spend the night on our boat and saw a light on inside," I told the patrolwoman as we walked down the dock. She shined her flashlight on the window of the cabin.

"Who's there?" the patrolwoman called out.

After a couple of seconds, the porthole opened. A very tall man swaggered out onto the top of the boat. The man had a happy smile and a friendly "Hello" as he blocked the light from the patrolwoman's flashlight with his hand. As my eyes adjusted, I recognized the man, and my heart filled with compassion. In spite of my exhaustion, *How could I not love my son?*

The patrolwoman led Jeff off the dock. He sat down on a patch of grass and stared off into space as if he were watching a movie on a big screen above the water.

"He's not supposed to be on our boat! He's court ordered to spend his nights in a sober living facility," I explained.

She replied, "Jeff's name is on the Boat User List on file in the Harbor office. He was here all day working on your boat. It's legal for him to be here. That is, unless you take him off the list." Jeff rocked back and forth, oblivious to the conversation.

"Can you arrest him for public intoxication?" I asked. I wanted him to be somewhere where he could sober up.

"No. He wasn't in public. He was in your boat until we asked him to get out," she replied.

So I called for a police dispatch. I hoped that the police might help because my son was court-ordered to be at a sober house.

The patrolwoman stared off into the bay as if this were a routine night. We waited over an hour and there was no sign of a dispatch. Jeff remained on the grass, knowing I had called the police on him. He continued swaying back and forth without a care.

The silence felt good. Jeff is comfortable with silence. A police car pulled up and the harbor patrol woman left.

Officer Landers listened as I said, "Jeff is court ordered to be at Freedom House—a few miles up the road, but I found him on our boat, high on something."

Officer Landers checked her computer and saw no warrant for Jeff's arrest. Then she spoke to Jeff in a motherly way, "Jeff, your mother doesn't want you on her boat. You need to find somewhere else to go tonight."

Like a lost child, Jeff stood up and wandered down the road until he disappeared.

PART TWO

CHAPTER THREE

In 1977, after three years of trying to have children without success, I took fertility pills. Soon, Greg and I suspected twins. It felt as if 8 limbs were kicking around inside of me. That was before ultrasounds were performed regularly. My doctor didn't suspect twins. My visits at the huge medical center were brief, and my doctor always found just one heartbeat.

At the time, I was a schoolteacher at Merryhill Elementary School in Sacramento, California while Greg was getting his PHD in physics at UC Davis. Some of my students would come up to me after school and put their hands on my belly, hoping to feel the baby kick. They squealed with delight when they felt any movement. On the last day of school, Greg picked me up outside my classroom door and we took a long awaited vacation to Southern California.

The six hour drive to visit our families was fun, with Greg making jokes that got me laughing as usual. After our arrival, Greg went to Disneyland with our relatives, but I opted out. Hours later, I felt an unusual cramping in my abdomen. I was seven months pregnant. I tried calling my doctor in Sacramento and also a local hospital. My doctor wasn't working that day and I was put on long holds. No one would tell me what to do, although they suggested I come in to be checked. Yet I didn't want to have my baby away from home. I wanted to know if I should drive home—hundreds of miles away. I called my big sister and asked her for a crash course on childbirth exercises. She told me to look up at the ceiling, focus on my breathing, and essentially, "zone out and relax." Not knowing if I was in labor or not, I packed to go home before Greg returned from Disneyland.

When we said goodbye to my parents in Simi Valley, my mother teased me for leaving so quickly. I suggested that twins might be in my big belly and Mom laughed, saying, "Big babies run in our family! It's false labor."

Greg and I ignored her and drove home in the night. When it hurt badly, I sang songs to myself for distraction.

When we finally walked into the Sacramento Kaiser Hospital's Labor and Delivery Department, a male receptionist greeted us. "You look like you're ready to pop," he said.

"I'm not due for two months," I replied.

A look of disbelief spread over his face. "That can't be. Your due date must be wrong!" he said.

"I took fertility pills," I replied. The next thing I knew, I was getting an x-ray of my belly. When we found out that we were going to have two babies we were elated!

I geared myself up for horrendous childbirth pain, but to my surprise, because the babies were small, the pain was less than I expected. Jeff's twin brother Tim came out first. The doctor called him Baby A and sent him off to the nursery. I said to myself, *The next one will be a girl.* We hadn't picked out boys names. I'd only picked out one girl's name because I wanted a girl. Then, with the help of forceps clamping on his head to give him a pull, Jeff came out.

My heart leaped with unexpected joy when I found out he was a boy. *Boys! Two boys! That's what I really wanted!*

The doctor whisked Jeff off to the nursery leaving me alone. I lay there smiling. When the doctor returned, he tried to tell me that Jeff was not going to make it. Jeff had hyaline membrane disease (underdeveloped lungs) which one of President John F. Kennedy's babies died from. I refused to believe that Jeff might not live. The doctor was upset that I wasn't taking him seriously. I was ecstatic, thinking, *Two babies! Not one!*

The doctor looked at me sternly, and I wiped the smile off my face to show I was listening. "Baby B has one chance in ten thousand to live," he said. I acknowledged that I heard him and he left. Yet I never believed him.

Through the porthole in his incubator, Jeff's tiny fist held my hand with a strong grip. His voice screamed a shrill cry when the physicians made me take my hand out so they could prick the sole of his foot with a needle to check the oxygen levels in his blood. After several weeks, Jeff was healthy enough to come home. Finally, both he and Tim could snuggle with us under our own roof anytime we wanted. Compared to school teaching, raising twins was easy. And for Greg, it was all fun and games.

Jeff had colic (bad stomachaches), but he stopped crying when Greg and I swung him and Tim through the air toward each other like airplanes about to crash. They squealed with delight as we changed course in midair, barely avoiding a collision.

Jeff loved music and would sway back and forth, mesmerized by Beethoven's symphonies. By the time he could talk, he was working the cassette player by himself, listening to Beethoven for several hours a day.

Our third son, Eli was born 21 months later. Tim and Jeff tried climbing on top of him, but I wouldn't let them. Once, when I wasn't looking, I heard Eli laughing. I came to see what was making him laugh and found Tim and Jeff on top of him in his crib, loving him. After that I let the boys play together, their toys spread out across our floor. At day's end we tidied house by scooping the toys into a corner with a garden rake.

When the twins were three, Christy was born. I pushed Tim, Jeff, Eli and Christy in our quadruple stroller all over the UC Davis campus. Our favorite excursion was our hike to Crocker Nuclear Lab. First, we passed our vegetable garden by the train tracks where the children squealed in delight when the noisy train rattled by. Next, we passed the hog farm, counting how many baby piglets were born since the last time we were there. Finally we arrived at the nuclear lab. There, Greg showed us the chambers where he ran experiments measuring protons and electrons which he shot through a tunnel and took pictures of.

The children loved to stop by the campus stream and duck pond on our way back from visiting Greg. The twins always climbed into an old abandoned boat left on dry ground. Shouting in glee, they pretended to be captains out on the sea.

Once, while nursing Christy in her room, I heard Tim excitedly shout from the bathroom. I went to see what was wrong, and found him sitting inside the toilet with his head sticking out and his arms outstretched above the water. He exclaimed, "Boat! Boat! Me in Boat!" There was never a dull moment. And the excitement continued after our little family of six moved to Simi Valley, California for Greg to work at Rocketdyne.

Jeff would throw spoons against the wall in the kitchen. "Ping!"
Greg would say, "Don't throw spoons against the wall."
"Ping!" went another piece of silverware against the wall.
"I thought I asked you to stop throwing spoons," Greg said.
"I'm not throwing spoons," Jeff replied. "Now, I'm throwing forks."

When Jeff learned to pray, he thanked God for flies, ladybugs, butterflies, beetles, electricity, light switches and a hundred other things. He never wanted to stop praying. Yet I had other children fussing for my attention. So I didn't hear him out.

Jeff asked Greg hundreds of questions.
"How far away is the moon?" Jeff asked.
In a heartbeat, Greg answered.
Then Jeff asked, "Why is the moon 240,000 miles away?"

Jeff started kindergarten a week after we had our fifth child, Butterfly. Eli nicknamed her after a butterfly-shaped cake that our neighbor gave us to celebrate her birth. We walked to school with the twins pushing Eli and Christy in a double stroller. I followed behind carrying Butterfly against my heart in a baby carrier.

In school, Jeff didn't interact with the other children. He stood back and watched them. He held his book upside down. His about-to-retire kindergarten teacher Mrs. Kowallis said that Jeff was "the most unusual child she'd ever met."

I read every book that the Simi Valley Library had on autism. Jeff fit the description to a "T"—except for one thing. Jeff talked. In the books back then, autistic kids were non-verbal.

Jeff's 1st grade teacher—a slender gray haired woman—was patient and kind. When Jeff jumped up and down on top of the classroom table, his teacher didn't lose patience. She seemed to understand he meant no harm. I later learned that autistic children have trouble understanding what is or is not socially acceptable. In addition, autistic children jump up and down to calm the horrendous confusion they live with in their brains.

Jeff's 2nd grade teacher had less patience. She said, "I don't care if Jeff learns nothing—except how to sit still in his seat and keep his hands to himself." Someone suggested we put Jeff on Ritalin—a medicine to calm hyperactivity. Yet Greg's brother Doug hadn't been allowed to attend elementary school unless he was on Ritalin. Doug said that taking Ritalin eventually led him to drug abuse. So we opted at that time to not have Jeff medicated.

When Jeff was seven, he went into a Resource Room with a special education teacher, Ms. Moreno. Jeff loved her fish aquariums, the peaceful uncrowded space to work in, and the one-on-one time he had with his teacher.

Jeff could not read, nor spell, nor learn his ABC's until he was 8-years-old. Also, he wet his bed every night. I tried not to embarrass Jeff over his bed wetting, and found encouragement over learning that my neighbor's sweet teenager daughter once had the same problem.

"My daughter wet the bed every night until she was eight-years-old," my neighbor told me. Then, when Jeff turned nine, he outgrew bedwetting too.

As Jeff advanced through school, no one could exactly identify what made Jeff different. Learning disabilities and emotional problems were discussed, yet Jeff's progress seemed to depend more on the teacher he had than on anything else.

Jeff's third-grade teacher, Mrs. Hogan held Jeff up as a shining example of a hard worker. She knew that Jeff had started doing his own laundry when he was five-years-old. He had no choice. With five children born

25

before the twins started kindergarten, the twins had to wash their own laundry or have no clean clothes to wear. They stood on a chair beside the washing machine, added clothes and soap, and pushed the buttons.

When Jeff was eight he learned his ABCs, and asked me to help him read one page from the Bible every night. I lay beside him on his bed— helping him sound out the words until my other children distracted me. It was hard to give him more time than my other children who were by then: Tim, Eli, Christy, Butterfly, and Phil.

Jeff still learned to read though—at an amazingly fast rate. Seemingly overnight, he learned to read at 3rd grade level. The next month he was at 4th grade level. The next month 5th, and so on. Soon he was reading college level textbooks about mechanics. However, he could only spell at second grade level.

When Jeff was 9-years-old, he went to an all-day special education class in a different school. There, he heard daily chants of "Retard, Retard, Retard," when he walked down the school hallway. Jeff's teacher told me he was unable to stop the verbal abuse because he was not always there when it happened.

At that school Jeff was regularly suspended for fighting—yet Jeff didn't fight. He was beat up. The school's policy was to suspend all participants in a fight. Yet with Jeff throwing no punches—even in self-defense—it wasn't fair. Kids would lay in wait for him and jump him. Jeff's nature is non-combative, which made him an easy target for cowardly bullies. I felt so frustrated and helpless each time Jeff was suspended, with the principal not listening to my arguments.

Jeff's Junior High school diagnosed him as being *Severely Emotionally Disturbed*. I took the diagnosis personally. Back then I had the habit of blaming myself when things went wrong.

Some of Jeff's teachers said that he was so smart that the only reason he didn't learn was because he didn't want to. Yet he tried harder than my other children. While the others played in our backyard after school, he spent hours trying to finish his homework. His favorite thing, though, was mechanics and our physical world. He noticed details in his surroundings, and learned how to tell what was wrong with a motor by listening to it.

Jeff loved to take broken things apart and fix them. Ever since he was old enough to walk down the street alone, he'd pull things out of people's trash containers—like broken tape recorders, radios, toasters, and clocks. He loved getting them to run. Soon I was driving him to the second-hand lawnmower store every week. There, he enjoyed looking at and purchasing motors.

Over time, I grew tired and impatient with the mess Jeff made in the garage. One day, I got rid of his mechanical collections while he was in school.

When Jeff came home and saw that everything was gone he said, "Didn't you know it's taken me years to collect all that stuff? Didn't you know some of the things you got rid of are irreplaceable? Didn't you know that what you threw out is worth a lot of money?" I covered up my conscience and tried to enjoy having a clean garage, but to this day I regret handling his mess with so much insensitivity.

When Jeff was 11, a man came to our home looking for a boy to deliver newspapers. He was looking for Tim. Tim wasn't home so Jeff offered to take the job. I thought Jeff couldn't handle the responsibility because he struggled in school. Yet Jeff insisted and I let him take the job. Over the years, Jeff was incredibly responsible for the deliveries. Yet he had trouble collecting money from customers. He patiently allowed many customers extra time to make late payments. After several months—when he concluded that they had no intention to pay—he stopped delivering to them and took money from his own salary to pay their unpaid bills.

Jeff used his salary toward raising fish. He had a dozen aquariums in our home. Among other fish, he raised difficult-to-breed gouramis and sold them to fish stores. One store owner said it was rare to find an adult who could raise those fish, not to speak of a child.

Jeff's 40 gallon aquarium in our living room was my favorite—with his black mollies, guppies, gouramis, neon tetras, miniature sharks, plecostomus, orange platties and zebra fish. When our last baby Matthew was born, I enjoyed feeding him in the night to the sound of the bubbling waters in that aquarium.

When Jeff was in 7th grade, his special education teacher, Ms. Chery gave him math work that was at the 10th and 11th grade levels. Although Jeff wasn't good at writing, there seemed to be nothing Jeff couldn't master in the way of math. He loved the success that he experienced in Ms. Chery's class. Then a school administrator said Jeff was too smart to be in Ms. Chery's class. He mainstreamed Jeff into regular classes and then explained Jeff's lack of success by calling it, "noncompliance." He suggested that Jeff was unable to function normally because of his parents, saying that I was high strung and Greg needed to spend more time with Jeff.

So Greg took up helping Jeff with his mechanical hobby. They bought a go kart assembly kit, worked together to get it running, and then made a go kart track in our backyard. When I look at old family videos, our destroyed landscape doesn't stand out as much as Jeff's beaming smile as he drives the cart.

Jeff continued to be unsuccessful in school. He would lie down on top of the classroom table or lose track of what assignments were given. When he began High School, he was placed in an all-day special education class with teachers who withheld privileges from him to try to make him do better in spelling. Jeff requested they give him harder math, but his teachers refused, saying, "He's fine in math. It's the other subjects we want him to work on."

Jeff looked forward to taking the high school Driver's Education Course, yet his teachers denied him the privilege. They said that his second-grade-level spelling skills were not good enough to merit him the privilege of driving.

Jeff found other ways to have fun. He lifted his new brother Matthew's infant carrier and swung it in a circle around our living room like an airplane on a string. Jeff grinned when I screamed for him to stop. Yet when I paused my screaming to take a breath, I heard baby Matt laughing!

Then one night, I had a dream. Part of my dream prompted me to more closely watch over my daughter Butterfly. Later, an earthquake came, and Butterfly was safe, by my side. As for Matt—whose life was in danger in my dream—I never left him unattended. With 6 teens and preteens, I had lots of distractions and errands to run. But I kept Matthew at my side.

In my dream, I also saw Jeff's special education bus coming to pick him up for school. There were no girls on the bus. Only the driver, a tall thin boy, and a short stout boy on the front seats. The bus stopped in front of our house and out of nowhere the children in Jeff's special education class appeared on our front lawn. They ran in circles around Jeff's special education teacher who stood contentedly with her hands folded in front of her. Then, Jeff walked out of our front door to board the bus. At that moment, a voice said, *Jeff doesn't belong with them.*

That morning, after my dream, Jeff was scheduled to take that bus for the first time. I told my children about my dream when they woke up. We waited together for his new bus. When it arrived it had no girls. Only the driver, the tall boy, and the short stout boy—just as I had seen in my dream.

The strange dream gave me courage to consider home schooling Jeff. I'd thought of it before, but lacked confidence. I finally gave Jeff the choice. He took me up on it.

Jeff was able to excel in math with Greg as his math and science teacher. His work study course was an apprenticeship at an auto mechanics shop. His favorite class was his parent-coached driver's training course.

Teaching home school drained my strength, so I hired Jeff to cook for our whole family, chalking up hours for his Home Economics course.

Frequently, Tim and Jeff made hamburgers to take to an old bum living behind our backyard in a shopping center. They delighted in climbing our backyard wall and delivering their delicious treats to the homeless guy. One New Year's Eve, though, on an especially cold night the old man died in his sleeping bag and the twins heard the sad news from the police who stood there by his empty camp.

Unfortunately, while eating donuts at Donut Inn at the shopping center, my sons met a man named Rob. Greg tried to warn me that he didn't like our boys seeing that man. Yet I was blind to there being any problem when the man took them boating, or for rides in his antique cars—including an antique fire engine. I didn't know that Rob was a child molester. Years later, I learned that Jeff was one of his victims. The shame that kids experience after being molested became Jeff's hidden wound.

Jeff turned 16 and used his paper route earnings to buy his first car. The 1960 Plymouth Duster cost only $200 and lasted only one week because Jeff drove onto the wrong side of a four-lane divided road. When he faced oncoming traffic, he realized his mistake and drove over the center divider to prevent an accident—which broke his axle. This didn't stop his automotive interests. From that point on, he bought one beloved car after another: dune buggies, Volvos, VW's, Datsuns, Toyotas, and a Karmann Ghia that he fit inside by curling his tall body nearly into a fetal position.

At age 17 Jeff was one class shy of graduating from Home High School when he lost interest in completing his classwork.

Jeff and Tim, as teenagers, had a drinking problem and were using illegal drugs. Greg and I asked the police for assistance when our boys started experimenting. Yet the police could do nothing to help. When the twins turned 18, I wanted them to move out. In fact, I moved out when Greg didn't kick the twins out on their 18th birthday. Matt was in day care at the time. A retired army drill sergeant ran the day care with his wife. One day the Sergeant asked me why I wasn't living at home. When I explained, he told me how to kick the twins out. He said, "Line up somebody from your church to come to your house in 10 days to remove all of their belongings. Then, tell the twins you're giving them a ten day's notice to move out. Tell them, 'You have ten days.' The next day, tell them, 'Nine days.' The next day, 'Eight.' And so on. Say nothing more."

I did as the Sergeant instructed. By the time I got down to "Three days," both Tim and Jeff were gone, and I moved back home.

Jeff moved in with his friend Ricky. Sometimes Jeff dropped by our home for canned goods for Ricky's household. Ricky's dad was a war veteran and an alcoholic. Ricky's grandfather was in a wheelchair. Jeff cared for the old man for years until he died.

Jeff was good at finding jobs. He worked on a farm giving pony rides to children. He bathed dogs at Canine Castle's dog grooming shop where he worked with his sister Butterfly. He washed three times more dogs per day than any other dog washer. People from all around brought unmanageable dogs to Jeff when no one else could handle them. Jeff moved home for a while when we got a Rottweiler puppy that would only let women and children approach it. All men in our house were growled at and nearly bitten except for Jeff; the Rottweiler treated Jeff like a child. In spite of Jeff's 6 ½ foot height, the dog never even barked at him.

At the age of 22, Jeff took the GED—the "General Education Development" Test. It certified his educational competency to be at High School graduate level and his math score was the highest score that the test administrator had ever seen.

Jeff continued to work at Canine Castle even after getting his court-order to live at Freedom House in 1999. He rode the train—a round trip of eighty miles a day—between Simi Valley and the beach town of Oxnard to get to his work at Canine Castle.

Later, Jeff drove his car to deliver newspapers early in the morning. When he invited me to go with him I was delighted, until he drove so fast on the sharp curves that I held my breath in fright. I decided to say nothing, though. After all, he did this every day and knew the route.

CHAPTER FOUR

There was a neighbor boy who used a walker to get around because he had cerebral palsy. He said Jeff was his best friend. Another boy who had Aspergers Syndrome waited every day for Jeff to come home from work and play video games with him, and he also felt Jeff was his best friend.

Once, Jeff brought home a bruised and broken friend of his, Olivia. She'd been thrown down the stairs by her former boyfriend and had a broken leg. I gave Olivia the room across from me. We talked to each other from across the hall, as I was sick in bed also. Olivia's life had been rough since her abused childhood, and we became good friends.

Jeff drove Olivia to visit her children who were in foster care. Olivia knew that Jeff formerly had a girlfriend with a baby that was not his—but Jeff loved the child as his own. Olivia told me, "Jeff is a special man to love another man's baby."

At one point I thought I was going to die from an undiagnosed sickness. I decided to quit fighting to live—and surrender to my sickness without a fight. It was then that Olivia told me that Jeff was crying because he thought I would die. She said, "Jeff was crying in your front yard when Greg came home from work. He said he felt like slugging his dad because he was against the type of medical help you wanted."

Greg hadn't wanted me to try alternative medical approaches because our insurance doctors had a reputation for being the best. Greg, as a scientist, trusted the traditional medical approach rather than the services of possible "quack doctors."

After hearing how upset Jeff was at the thought of losing me, I became proactive—ignoring all costs—in preserving my life through alternative health care. It made a difference. If it weren't for Jeff's tears, I feel I wouldn't be alive.

Later, Jeff and Olivia moved out and rented rooms from a friend. Olivia eventually became entrenched in alcohol and illegal drugs and found another boyfriend, Jose. Yet she still called on Jeff whenever she wanted money.

One evening, I saw Jeff typing a letter on the computer to someone. Around that time, Olivia had conceived another child and moved with her boyfriend Jose to Puerto Rico. Here's the letter that Jeff typed. He used spell check to help him out.

> Iv had allot of free time recently and if I'm smart id like to use it to go back to school they have some automotive classes and maybe Sunday would be interested in owning MI own business
>
> Some people actually make a living by selling and buying cars and I would like to look into that moor
>
> Until recently I was spending all of my time and efforts trying to help a friend...a girl... though some of the things she's done make me wonder if she really was a friend...
>
> ...she has lupus... I guess it is not a fun thing to have anyway it made her sick allot and hard to keep down a job thou I think it woos as much if not moor her drinking problem about a month and half ago I helped her and her new boyfriend move to Puerto Rico

I hope the best four her but something had to change she always needed something and it took every minute I had now I have time to spend on myself thou I donut know riley what to do I guess iv bin living four other people four so long maybe in part because it took me away from my own problems and kept me away from fear and regret of the past

I cherished having Jeff live at home while Olivia was in Puerto Rico. He bought and repaired broken down cars. There was nothing he couldn't fix. One Sunday after church a man couldn't get his car started. Three people tried helping him, yet gave up and left. I called Jeff who was at home and told him about the problem. In two minutes he was at the church, barefoot, in Levis with holes in the knees, fixing the car. He got it running in no time, using only a rubber band and a piece of tape.

Jeff sent Olivia and her boyfriend Jose money every month throughout her pregnancy because Jeff thought he might be the father of the baby. When Olivia came back to California just in time to give birth, Jeff and I were there at the hospital. The baby girl looked like me and we included Olivia in our family circle so long as Jose was out of the picture; he was in jail most of the time. Jeff got an apartment for Olivia, himself, and the baby in 2003, making every effort to make her comfortable. Later, when Jose got out of jail, Olivia kicked Jeff out of the apartment. Although Jeff had signed a six-month lease, Olivia refused to let him get his belongings. Then, vandalism and a fire ruined everything. All of Jeff's belongings were gone, including his valuable camera which he had filled with pictures of Hawaii on a trip he enjoyed with Greg, Phil, Matt and me, a few months before.

Around that time, Jeff had $3,000 that he saved while working at Canine Castle. Yet, because of his efforts to provide for Olivia's needs, Jeff was going downhill financially. Olivia took Jeff's debit card and shared it with people that Jeff didn't know. Jeff, who prided himself on saving money and spending wisely, had difficulty recovering.

In spite of the deep hurt he felt, he continued helping Olivia and her baby. When she became homeless several times, he found places for them to live and paid the bill. He stayed up all night—after working all day—to fix his car so that he could drive Olivia and her baby to visit her other children in their foster care homes. He later discovered through a paternity test that Olivia's child, who he cared for and loved, wasn't his.

Olivia wanted more and more money from Jeff. She called our home at all hours of the night to rant and cuss at Jeff. On occasion, she came to our home and yelled at him in front of me. He wasn't even her boyfriend. Olivia's drama and cussing made me sick.

Once, when she used our bathroom, jewelry was missing afterward. It was then that I got a restraining order that forbid she have contact with me in my home. It stopped her from ringing our house phone in the night and waking me up with her ranting and cussing. Olivia lost the little girl that Jeff had loved. Social Services took the child away from her due to her drug and alcohol abuse.

Jeff took it hard that Olivia lost her child even though he wasn't the father.

Like me, Jeff needed vacations out in nature in order to heal. Our family often took vacations to Southern Utah where we delighted in the rivers, waterfalls, and red rock canyons. Jeff and I also began taking road trips. Just the two of us.

We'd park the van under a shade tree by a stream. I'd read, and Jeff would put up his feet to ease the pain of going without alcohol. A quiet and peaceful time.

Once, on our way home from visiting Southern Utah, Jeff and I casually conversed as I drove 70 miles per hour on the Pear Blossom Highway. The desert whizzed by as Jeff finished telling me a story about someone who had gotten lost in the desert and died of exposure and dehydration. I started to express my hope for people to find comfort in the face of their misfortunes. I mentioned Olivia's name, aiming to express my hope that she will turn out alright in the end; she had a good heart.

I barely got her name out of my mouth, though, when Jeff exploded. He cried as his arm swung out toward the windshield. He was mortified when he saw the shattered glass. More frustrated than ever, he unfastened his seat belt. I slammed on the brakes and came to a halt as Jeff bolted out of the car and ran off into the desert barefoot.

I sat in the driver's seat crying and praying for Jeff, as I thought of the people Jeff told me about who got lost in the desert and died.

Suddenly, a policeman came up to my car window. I hadn't seen a police car. I was surprised, yet thankful. I told the policeman what had happened and he set out on foot to find Jeff.

After a long wait I saw the policeman and Jeff walking together as if they were good friends. They got to my car and the policeman said, "We had a nice talk. Do you feel safe driving home with Jeff in your car?"

I turned to Jeff and asked, "Would you agree to attend an AA meeting as soon as we get back to Simi Valley?"

Jeff replied, "Yes."

"We'll be fine," I told the officer. Jeff hadn't been drinking but I hoped the AA meeting would help in some way—it was the only available support I could think of.

Butterfly married Dragonfly, a man with a nickname to go along with Butterfly's name. While Dragonfly was stationed overseas in the army, Butterfly lived in Simi Valley, with Jeff as her house guest. It was during that time that Butterfly's first child was born. Shortly after, the wildfires came. Butterfly's house was located at the edge of ten thousand acres of brush-covered hills. I'd been in Utah visiting my mother when the fires came. While sleeping, I had a vivid dream where I saw Butterfly's house in the night with flames shooting up three times higher than the house.

I quickly drove home in the night. As I approached the mountain pass which leads to Simi Valley, I was in awe over the magnificent red glow of the sky. I'd never seen anything like it. Although destructive, I was mesmerized by the powerful fire coming down the west hills of Simi Valley. I went straight to Butterfly's house which had been evacuated. Jeff stood on the roof with a hose. When he saw me, he called out, "Get another hose!" I quickly drove home and returned with the hose. Jeff used two hoses to make so much water flow off of Butterfly's roof that there was a moat going around her house. The fire fighters saw the waterfalls streaming down the edges of the roof. They left Jeff alone while they tended the neighbor's homes.

The fire was phenomenal—the whole mountain behind Butterfly's house was in a blaze so high, so bright, and so immense that I stood in absolute awe. Then I realized that my greatest fear had passed. The fire burned everything up to Butterfly's yard, including her fence, but not her house. I remembered that my dream hadn't shown her home engulfed by flames—but silhouetted by them. I had misinterpreted my dream. Yet it got me home to fetch Jeff a hose. After the danger passed, I retreated home and found Butterfly, her baby, and Greg asleep. Only Jeff remained at Butterfly's house on the roof with the hose after I went to bed.

Before the next summer, Dragonfly had returned home from the army and Butterfly, now expecting another baby, asked Jeff to move out. He had been using drugs and alcohol which made her nervous.

Jeff was living away from home and walking down the street in ragged clothes, barefoot and dehydrated from the summer heat. He stopped to drink from someone's front yard hose while carrying a pet snake that he'd found in the gutter. He tenderly held his snake like a baby bird and was talking to it. Then, against his will, the police came and took him to a mental hospital on a 72-hour hold—a forced hospitalization for which Jeff was billed over $10,000. Jeff had no savings, yet he had never been in debt. He was angry that he was forced to be hospitalized and then given the bill.

Shortly after, Jeff was put in the hospital with another 72 hour hold to recover from excessive drug and alcohol use. Upon his release, a member of the hospital staff drove Jeff to our front porch and instructed him to stay home where it was safe, and to not go back to the hills where he had been camping. Jeff stayed with us for a week before returning to the hills. I thought he might have left because I was stressed over something. I thought my stress affected him and made him want to drink. We allowed no drinking in our home because of the craziness of substance abuse, and the way it wrenched our lives with trauma. Greg and I located countless rehabs for Jeff to go to, to no avail.

Jeff's trips to jail added up. Public intoxication. Resisting arrest. Possession of a controlled substance. He lived in various places—in our home, in the woods, and in his car. Once, while sleeping in his car he was bitten by a brown recluse spider. The wound filled with puss which he drained by the cupful. He came home and stayed with us for a few days. He cared more about his wound than about his alcohol and drugs. It was a delight to have him home. Then, Greg and I had an argument about some little thing that had nothing to do with Jeff. Jeff left that day for his life out in nature, parked under a tree.

Before long, Jeff was living under a bridge in the nearby town of Thousand Oaks where he landed a job at Indiana Bones Temple of Groom. He had lost his car, so was happy to make a camp by the grooming shop. About that time, I read about a rattlesnake crawling inside a man's sleeping bag while the man slept. When the man awoke, he didn't kill it. Instead he said, "We had a nice nap together." The story reminded me of the type of man Jeff is.

Not long after, Jeff joined us for a family picnic. Afterward, Greg and I dropped him off at his bridge. Intrigued, I watched Jeff walk through a dense thicket by the bridge in the black of night. I marveled at how brave he was as he disappeared in the dark all alone. He mentioned hearing a rattlesnake in the bushes by his camp, to warn me to be careful if I visited him.

By daylight I came to his camp and was impressed. He kept a plastic bottle next to a hillside sprinkler head with a constant drip, for collecting drinking water. He also hung a large water bottle from the branch of a nearby tree to be heated by sunlight and used for showers. I noticed how lonely, yet peaceful and serene his camp was. His home there consisted of a tarp, with a folded sleeping bag on it, beside a stack of newspaper ads for cars and boats for sale. I met him there regularly and took him to a restaurant where we discussed boats for sale.

His home under the bridge didn't last long. He went to jail frequently for public intoxication and missed too many days of work.

The years that followed are a blur. Yet my diary tells part of the story.

On September 16, 2004 I wrote: I walked up to our front door and found Jeff asleep, curled up like a kitten on our porch. He woke and asked for socks and food. I let him come in to get them. Now, Jeff's gone, and I'm lying on a lounge outside, troubled. My heart is hard—afraid to be soft. Round after round, Jeff gets sober and moves home, and then breaks something. He made holes in the walls with his fist; he slugged and cracked the glass of our front door twice. He tore one door off its hinges. Not long ago while he was living at home, I asked him to clean his room and he broke his bedroom window with his fist.

In November of 2004, I wrote: I went to the homeless shelter to sleep because every time I fell asleep at home, someone woke me up for something trivial—like to ask how to spell a word or to ask me where the stapler was. After I'd been awakened from exhausted sleep by my children three times, I was so angry that I wanted to bust a window. Not long before that I had slugged our old TV. Although the TV didn't break, I sprained my wrist.

Now I felt volatile again. I prayed, *God help me to not break a window.* God answered, *You are too tired to be strong.* It was then that I decided to sleep at the homeless shelter.

I walked into the church where the homeless slept, and was delighted to see Jeff. We enjoyed hot chocolate and donuts as we talked together.

Later that night, Jeff was sleeping in the men's half of the shelter. I slept in the women's half and awoke when I heard a noise which broke my heart. Jeff was crying in his sleep.

Once a homeless person left his belongings in our yard and did not come back for them. I discarded what could easily be replaced and saved what was valuable—like this poem. I never found out who wrote it, but it sounds like something Jeff would write:

I don't rilly care what I look like.
I'd be happy if I was a rock and you were
A flower growing out of a crack in me.
And every time a bee tried to steal your honey, we could eat it.

And eventually everyone would just leave us alone.
Then you could put your head down and I would too.
And we could sleep.
And I wud know that you are there.

CHAPTER FIVE

In 2004, Jeff was still living away from home most of the time. For a while, he slept near our home in a wooded area by the shopping center. Tim and I brought him food when he came to our back wall, and visited with him. One day, Jeff told me that in the woods where he slept, a raccoon came within a few feet of his sleeping bag. "I was going to coax it to come closer, but I hear they can be mean," he said. That was the only time I remember him being afraid to get close to an animal.

Another time when we were visiting over our backyard wall, Jeff proudly announced, "I'm six days sober." Then it was, "Seven." Then, "Eight." Then, "Nine."

The next day, Jeff went to Simi Valley Mental Health Services to get help with insomnia. The prescription they gave him seemed to take the edge off his self-control. He never made it sober to ten days.

Once we invited Jeff to visit with us on our patio. There, he pulled out a dollar bill and a pack of matches from his pocket. He lit the money on fire, and while holding the dollar bill in front of his face, he watched it burn and sang, "Happy Birthday to you." When he's drunk he can be so stupid and think it's funny.

Around that time I had my second brain tumor. My doctor said that it was only a small tumor and that the medicine should help. Yet the medicine was making my pain worse. It kept me awake all night and made me feel like someone was pouring acid on my brain. I quit taking the medicine and found pain relief out in nature. I began living in my van by the beach to help me manage my pain.

One day, while resting by the pounding surf, feeling the spray of water on my face and the earth rumble under my body, I heard a voice speak in my mind. *Go to Utah,* It told me. I decided to go to Utah to heal and invited Jeff to go with me if he'd promise to stay sober. He promised, and together we went to the town where his great-great-grandpa's house still stands.

On the way there, driving through the snow in Zion National Park, Jeff showed me his fingers, swollen from frostbite, "I fell asleep one night behind the Jack in the Box by the train tracks," he said. "It got real cold and when I woke up, my fingers were frozen." Soon his fingers would begin to heal.

Orderville is a small town of 400 people, nestled between three national parks: The Grand Canyon, Bryce Canyon, and Zion. In that little town, the sun lingers just beyond the horizon for several hours each morning and evening, hidden by the mountains. Clouds sail through the sky in unpredictable patterns, glowing with silver linings, or rumbling with thunder and looming in darkness. There, everyone waves to us when we pass—whether they know us or not. It is our ancestral town where half of the people in the cemetery are related to us.

In Orderville, we first rented the Walker's cottage—a barn converted into a guest house. When Jeff was a child, a colt was born there. Our first hour in Orderville, Jeff played in the pasture with the same colt—grown into a stallion. Then Jeff explored the hills and found our landlord's teenage daughter and her friends with their car stuck in the mud. He helped them get their car out of the rut and made a good impression. Too good. Our landlord said she felt nervous about her teenage daughter becoming infatuated with Jeff and she asked us to move out.

On January 1, 2005 Jeff and I began staying at the Parkway Motel, which I nicknamed The River Cottage after the Virgin River that flows behind it. That first night, Jeff bicycled 10 miles in the snow to buy a six-pack from a distant gas station. He was then considerate enough to leave the 5 unused cans on our front porch when he went to bed. I threw the cans away because of our agreed-upon-no-booze-rule. My approach was no nonsense: "This is the way it is." And Jeff began his recovery.

For a month, Jeff couldn't get out of bed due to the depression that naturally accompanies one's withdrawal from alcohol. Then, Jeff heard me in the kitchen one day while I was preparing a care package for his cousin Diane who needed food. He got out of bed to see what I was doing. "This isn't good enough. She needs more," he said. Then he got dressed and went to the store for tuna, beans, pasta and nuts. After filling the box to the brim, he took it to the post office and mailed it for me. Then, he volunteered to remove the drywall next door where they were renovating a historical building. He also started attending church, recovery meetings, and looking for a job.

The first job that Jeff applied for was at Best Friends Animal Sanctuary, a former movie ranch in Kanab, Utah. There, John Wayne movies were filmed alongside the cliffs, canyons, and rivers.

Jeff took me on a tour of the Animal Sanctuary. We played with a 23-year-old Appaloosa which had formerly weighed in at only 400 pounds. We toured 'Dog Town Heights' and 'Kitty Hotel,' where 12,000 abandoned pets were housed.

Later Jeff and I picnicked in a shady grotto with waters cascading out of a rock. The feeling there was magical. Peaceful. Then, Jeff and I drove further into the canyon, parked our van, and hiked—each going in different directions. Jeff told me after we finished hiking that he had slipped while jumping over a chasm twenty feet above the icy river. "I was doing the splits to try to get myself out!" he said. How relieved we were that he made it out alive! Then we started to drive home but got stuck in the mud. The spinning tires created a muddy rut in the canyon. Jeff silently watched me maneuver, as if amused. When I asked for his help, he knew exactly how to turn the wheels to get us unstuck.

Back in Orderville, I got a job as a substitute teacher in a kindergarten class. It was my first chance to teach school since before Jeff was born. Jeff listened to my lesson plans and cheered me on saying, "You can do it!"

Jeff initially found no work in Utah, although he applied at Best Friends Animal Sanctuary twice. However, Canine Castle in California called him to fill in for an employee going on vacation. Jeff agreed to take the job and took a bus to California. He went to the hills to live the night before his work began. The next day, he showed up for work high on Crystal Meth.

Within minutes, he was throwing machinery around and beating his head against the wall, blood flowing from his mouth and nose. Then he struggled with the police when they came to take him to jail.

From jail, Jeff called me to make plans for his return to Utah after his time was served. He often shared things like, "I did 300 pushups in jail today, and 400 sit ups!"

Later, he told me he was losing weight because the jail wasn't feeding him enough. I gave him food money for every chapter in the Bible he copied. He copied by hand the entire books of Genesis, Psalms, Proverbs, Jeremiah, John, and Revelations—along with the books that had his brothers' names: Philippians, Timothy, and Matthew. I sent him extra food money and he stopped losing weight. Plus, the writing he did in jail improved his spelling.

By spring, Jeff had served his time for his intoxication charge. He was released. He had yet another charge for having scratched an officer in the scuffle during his arrest. The sentencing for that was postponed for a year.

When Jeff returned to Orderville, the townspeople welcomed him home. Our pastor, Bishop Reese said, "Take lots of hikes in the mountains. This is a good place to heal." We drove up a dirt road called The Muddy— leading to lakes and cliffs far away from civilization. We had to brake for a hundred deer walking across the road. Then, we explored hidden canyons, hidden lakes, and a very old trailer with cupboards full of rodent droppings and feral kittens who hissed at us like lion cubs.

Our landlord at the River Cottage sold me a rust-colored Nissan truck for $275 which I let Jeff drive. Together we made our own roads up steep hillsides.

One day, we drove to Cedar Mountain after a storm to visit the hidden lakes, lava caves, and waterfalls. Quail ran out of the bushes when we drove by. Deer leaped into the thicket. Canyon vistas took my breath away. When we came to fallen trees blocking our path, we made our own roads or got out and moved tree limbs. We delighted in visiting Navajo Lake where Jeff as a child went boating with his grandpa.

At the river cottage all was fine until tourist season began. Our landlord needed our cottage for her nightly tourist rentals and asked us to find another place to live. We found no housing in town so we moved to a beautiful campground beside The Muddy. There, we watched brilliant sunsets and lightning storms. Jeff slept in the Nissan truck. I slept in my van where I enjoyed playing my guitar and watching a little hummingbird which flew in and out of my van.

I worked as a waitress all day while Jeff read books in the truck with the hatch open. His body healed from drug abuse while reading mystery novels—surrounded by magnificent scenery and fresh mountain air. Eventually, we found a fixer upper to rent—formerly nicknamed the haunted house. With Jeff's help, I turned the old place into a home. We delighted in finding a free washing machine that leaked only a bit when we ran it, a free canary, a couch, and a bed from an elderly farmer who said we could borrow it if we didn't pee on it.

I let Jeff borrow my Nissan truck to drive over 70 miles of winding roads to St. George, Utah. There, he visited his maternal grandma, and he found work with Labor Ready, an employment company that sent him out on construction jobs.

After his first day at work, someone offered him a beer, but he refused saying, "No thanks! I'm going to visit my grandma."

In no time, Jeff landed a job at the St. George Steel Mill. His boss told him on his first day of work, "I don't bother to learn my employees' names until they've been here a few months. Nobody sticks with the job." Yet

Jeff stayed on and ended up supervising the work of 50 men who worked under his direction.

Although Jeff was well-liked at work, he had no friends outside the workplace. When he called me on the phone from St. George, he'd be parked under a freeway overpass in the desert, with his voice slurring. Someone told me that Jeff would only stay sober while working in St. George if he had a friend. "Just one good friend," the person said.

> Drugs block the pain, the drink hides away
> The fears we can't face, the things we can't say:
> Our yearning to heal, our yearning to love,
> Our hope for a place that we feel a part of.

I read that experiments with rats proved they do better when they are not alone. When a rat is given a choice between plain water and water with heroin in it, it drinks mostly heroin water when it's isolated. However, when a rat is placed in a Disneyland-like cage with lots of other rats, it drinks mostly water. Jeff did better living with me in Orderville than on his own in Saint George.

Once he showed me the place where he liked to park and sleep by a dry stream bed. He pointed at some rocks and said, "I saw a rattlesnake at the bottom of this dry waterfall."

I missed Jeff when he was at work. He only stayed in our fixer upper on the weekends. He brought a few beers with him, but I didn't say anything. I felt impressed to just love him. To encourage sobriety, we took lots of drives through the mountains with him behind the wheel.

On one rutted ledge in Zion National Park, Jeff drove the truck while playing a CD of music Matthew had given me for Christmas. As Beethoven's Seventh Symphony played, I was so frightened by Jeff's driving that I closed my eyes, praying that we would not crash before we reached the summit. Once there, I opened my eyes, overlooking a stupendous view of endless mountains spread out before us.

On another occasion, Jeff's driving frightened me and I asked him to let me out of the truck. I waited in a meadow, and when he didn't come back, I envisioned him bleeding at the bottom of a cliff. I said to myself, *I'd pray for his bleeding to stop while hiking for help.* After what seemed like forever, Jeff drove back all smiles.

Eventually, Jeff bought a Harley Davidson from the year he was born—1977—for $200. His alcohol use continued, but I tried to remain calm.

Later, Jeff found an ad for a boat for sale. We drove my van to Parowan, 65 miles away, to look at it. The monstrous wooden boat was dilapidated, and Jeff didn't want it. On our way back to Orderville, we noticed a dry lakebed that begged to be explored. Dirt roads were everywhere. Driving too fast on one of the roads, we took an unexpected dip. With a big jolt, the ball joint of my van's right wheel broke. My van literally bit the dust.

We walked a mile to the nearest house where we met a woman named Kaiki, a woman who was in recovery from having a brain tumor removed. Kaiki thought her tumor had been caused by an accident she had on that same road that broke our ball joint. Her car had rolled three times.

Kaiki was the second person I'd met with a brain tumor. The other person was a man undergoing chemotherapy. He looked less healthy than Kaiki who opted for a nutritional flush over chemo. She encouraged me to trust in nutritional flushes for my own tumor and boosted my faith in natural approaches.

As for the van biting the dust—Jeff felt bad that he wasn't driving slower, but I was glad for the chance to meet Kaiki—a sympathetic person to talk with about my health concerns.

Also—as part of my tumor treatment—I signed up for the St. George Marathon. Endorphins released during exercise can heal brain tumors, research suggests.

The day for the marathon finally arrived. My van was repaired, and I left Orderville, driving toward St. George. I parked my van to take a nap in Zion, and discovered that my van wouldn't start when I woke up. A park ranger came, gave me a jump start, and 30 miles later, my engine died again on a steep mountain road. I coasted downhill to a gas station, got another jump start and continued on.

When I reached the city of Washington, Utah, my van stopped again and wouldn't restart. I called Jeff. He left his night shift at the Steel Mill and helped me get my van towed to a St. George repair shop. He drove me to the convention center just minutes before they closed, and I picked up my packet for the morning marathon. Then, I asked Jeff to drop me off at the repair shop parking lot where I planned to sleep in my van. I caught a wink of sleep while Jeff went back to working at the Steel Mill. At 3 AM, he returned to take me to the location where the runners boarded buses for the starting place. Once at the starting place, I enjoyed bonfires, and the excitement which filled the air, while Jeff resumed working.

When Jeff finished his night shift, he waited 6 ½ hours until I finished the 26 mile race. His happy smile greeted me at the finish line. My smile faded when someone said to Jeff, "Why don't you grow up?" I didn't know what the person was referring to, but to me, Jeff was my hero, going without sleep for over 24 hours so I could live a dream come true—my first marathon.

On our way back to Orderville, Jeff and I camped off road near Zion. Jeff guided me away from a spot on the river where a lot of campers were crazy drunk and led me to a quiet spot.

Later, we picked up my dog Jonny who I'd left with a friend, and ate dinner at the Spotted Dog Café. I feared my dog would not be welcome at the ritzy restaurant, yet with Jonny sitting on Jeff's lap, a magic permeated the place. Even the waiter was enthralled with our spotted dog at the Spotted Dog Café.

At the end of 2005, the river cottage became available again. I was glad to leave the fixer upper because my landlord there tried to hit on me—something that Jeff had warned me to watch out for. When that landlord crossed the line of decency, I hurled angry words at him about wishing he'd get struck by a bolt of lightning, and I was gone within a day—back to the river cottage.

Come December, I was spending more and more time in Zion National Park while Jeff was working overtime in St. George. At Zion, I napped in a meadow one day and woke to see a dozen deer grazing around me, including a buck with big antlers. They took little notice of me as I edged my way to a ledge above them to admire their beauty and write in my diary.

In January 2006, Jeff was charged with a felony for having scratched a police officer early in 2005, at the Canine Castle incident. It was an emotional moment when I drove Jeff to jail, passing through St. George on our way. His boss at St. George Steel had written a letter to the California courts recommending they let Jeff off due to his outstanding work at the Steel Mill. It was to no avail.

As we passed the Steel Mill, Jeff cried out, "I could run! I don't want to go to jail! I could just stay! I could just stay!!" With that, he slugged the side window of the van and I cried, *God, help us.* It didn't break, and a warm comfort enveloped me as I felt God say, *Things will get better.*

When Jeff came home, fresh out of jail sober, he, Tim, and I flew to Kentucky. There we visited Butterfly, Dragonfly, and their small children. At Kentucky Lake on the Cumberland River, a storm pelted down on our boat. All the other boats left but we waited out the storm. The sunshine returned, and oh the love and the laughter we shared tubing, fishing, and swimming.

The trip would have been much different if it weren't for Jeff. At the beginning, when we drove out of the Nashville airport toward Butterfly's house, we entered an area with steep cliffs on both sides. Tim fell asleep at the wheel. He later said that the last thing he remembered was adjusting his seat and thinking, *Oh, how comfortable this feels!* I was asleep on the backseat and Jeff was in the passenger seat beside Tim. Suddenly, going 75 mph, we veered toward the edge of the cliff and with a sudden cry, Jeff yelled, "What are you doing?" He grabbed the wheel and corrected our disastrous course.

CHAPTER SIX

Jeff made a difference in dramatic and sometimes quiet ways back home in Simi Valley.

Once, Jeff came down from the hills to get water, but was arrested for not showing up in court. The next day I picked him up from jail and offered to bring him home.

"I don't want to go home," he replied, "I need to take water to my friends." He asked me to drop him off where he'd been arrested near the AM/PM market. He got out of the van, walked to some bushes behind the store, fetched his empty water jug, and without a word filled it up with water and headed back to the hills.

Later, Jeff lived at home and looked on Craig's List for tools and cars. He pointed out a car he'd like to buy for me, a bike he wanted for Dad, a dirt bike for Matthew, and a family boat. After a few days at home, Jeff would leave again. I picked up the pieces he left behind. Memories. Here's one, a job resume:

I most recently worked at St. George Steel. My duties included maintenance and repair of sand blasting equipment, sand blasting...

Also working in extreme weather conditions (115 degrees Fahrenheit summer, and 15 degrees Fahrenheit winter)

Previous employment includes five years dog grooming…

Six months automotive shop apprentice as a teenager;

Six months work with farm animals and children at Party   Animals Petting Zoo;

Five years paper route as a pre-teen and teenager;

Construction, delivery, and misc. jobs.

I am currently looking for long term employment with a company that will appreciate my talents, give me a sound financial foundation, and be a good work experience.

I took Jeff back to Utah hoping it would bring some stability to his life. It was then that I discovered that Spirits—or alcohol—affect me like secondhand smoke.

While in Utah, Jeff had a buddy who he liked to drink with at night after Jeff's construction jobs were done. They drank down by the river behind our cottage.

Back in the 90's when I was treated for mental illness, I suffered side effects from medications. I'd hear things that weren't real: a herd of horses running through my house, a witch cackling, repeated knocks on the door, and evil hateful voices. After I quit taking my medicine, the hallucinations went away—until Jeff and his buddy started drinking down by the river. His buddy was from a loving family, yet, like Jeff, he had a weakness for alcohol. I would see their beer cans by the shore the next morning, along with some mail the boy had left behind. I glanced at a letter and saw it was from his grandparents telling him how much they loved him.

Yet Jeff and his friend repeatedly drank by the river at night, and I'd repeatedly hear voices. The voices woke me from my sleep, saying in a mean and taunting voice, "Come down to the river." When Jeff came back into our cottage, I pleaded with him to stop drinking, "Your drinking makes me hear voices. Don't drink!"

Yet his weakness went on until his friend went to jail. Then the drinking and the hallucinating stopped. A few weeks passed. Then, we decided to return to California.

Back in California, Jeff begged me to take him back to Utah. When I was delayed, he decided to attend church with his brothers Tim and Phil. While there, he heard about some people having a party. His brothers were invited, but Jeff wasn't. The hostess was nervous about inviting Jeff because he had just gotten out of jail. My heart broke. We believe in not judging and being kind. Yet Jeff couldn't go to the party and my job was to deal with it humbly.

That night, after Jeff was unsuccessful at finding a way to get to the party, he reluctantly took a painting job at Rob's house. Rob was the man who molested Jeff as a child and his house was the last place that Jeff wanted to go. Yet that Sunday night, Jeff accepted the painting job.

When Jeff's painting was done, he came home angry because Rob hadn't paid him. I thought maybe Jeff had been paid in drugs, because he was agitated. He stormed through our house, angry. Then he went through the front door, stumbled over a bike left on our porch, and when he got up off the ground, flung it aside—through our living room window.

Jeff had only been out of jail for 3 days when he was arrested and sent back. The more he stayed in California, the worse things got.

Jeff wanted to return to our empty river cottage each time he got out of jail. He asked a dozen times for me to take him back to Utah, yet I found it hard to leave the rest of my family.

About that time, Tim and Phil had time on their hands during their summer vacation from college. I kicked them out of our California home and asked them to find jobs in Orderville—and to take Jeff with them. Phil complained about moving to Utah and Jeff complained about Phil's complaints. Tim got a job as a server at a rustic mountain restaurant.

Later, I joined them and the four of us drove to the Grand Canyon together. We hiked the north rim under a cloudy sky, while tourists played their guitars on the trail and lightning brilliantly illuminated the canyon.

We watched the storm and ate hamburgers in a restaurant that had 20 foot high windows. Then we headed back to Orderville and discovered a fire tower on the way. We climbed up the tower's 600 steps, pretending we were spotting forest fires, shouting out, "Over there! Lightning just hit the tree on the top of that hill!"

The next day we hiked up The Narrows in Zion Canyon. The Narrows are where the Virgin River flows between cliffs that are a thousand feet high. Tim, Phil, Jeff and I floated down the river, laughing and playing. We jumped off high rocks into the water and floated face down, pretending we were dead.

Later, I rested alone on a picnic blanket by the river and a skunk walked out of the woods toward me. I started singing so the skunk wouldn't be startled and spray me upon discovering I was near, yet my singing didn't distract him. He kept walking toward me and got right on my picnic blanket with me. I sat still with my heart pounding until he finally meandered off to the stream.

At summer's end, back in California, Jeff began living in the hills more than at home. He said, "I have my own home. I have a tent, a garden, a dog, and a water hole."

Once Jeff came home with black eyes and bruised cheeks.

"What happened?" I asked.

"Someone was beating up his girlfriend so I stopped him," he replied. Then he added, "I'll stay at home for a few days to let things settle down."

This experience repeated itself again and again, as well as his return trips to jail.

I wrote in my diary one night:

I walked into Jeff's empty room repeatedly during the night
Wishing he was there.
With every noise I heard,
I went to look for Jeff.
Nothing.

At the crack of dawn I wrote: I panic upon waking and realizing that the night is over and Jeff never came home. He had joined our family for dinner in his quiet way. He had seemed distant, until he did a double take when Greg told a story:

There was a flea bitten horse that nobody bought at an auction. On its way to the slaughterhouse, a man rescued the sickly horse. He took it home, naming it "Snowflake." Later, Snowflake won every jumping competition it entered in the USA.

Greg made his point, saying, "When you think you're of no value, you still are."

The look on Jeff's face was incredulous as Greg said, "Your life has value beyond what you perceive. If you think your life has no value, you are wrong."

I read on in my diary: Now I walk outside looking for Jeff on our patio swing. It's just swaying in the wind. I think of my home filled with love— and of how my children touch my heart. Even Jeff, in his misery, reaches out humbly to give love. I'm happy. Yet I'm grieving. *God, bring Jeff home.*

On a rainy night I wrote in my diary: At midnight I heard the gate open. Wondering if it was Jeff, I walked into the back yard where Jeff had left some blankets. They were wet and surrounded by rain puddles. Suddenly, the sprinklers came on under my feet, but they didn't startle me. All I cared about was Jeff. I walked to our driveway, peered through the window of my van in the dark and saw a sleeping form. He was there.

At dawn I brought Jeff food, clothes, and water. He spoke of suicide and I told him I loved him. 'If it weren't for you, a lot of people—including me—wouldn't be alive. Life is for learning, which requires we go through painful times. Yet the pain will pass. Praying helps,' I said. Jeff replied, 'I've been praying all day.'"

Jeff was delighted when Mother's Day came and we had a family dinner—until he noticed that his brother Eli wasn't there. Concerned, he asked to borrow my phone. The next thing we knew, Eli was coming to Mother's Day dinner for the first time in 12 years!

Another Mother's Day approached and Jeff walked 5 miles with a sore leg to meet Greg and me, to go on a sailing trip. Yet, by the time he arrived, I'd become ill and called off sailing. I suggested we drop Jeff off at the dock to live on our boat and sober up. But it shook Jeff's world to not go sailing. "I can't live on the boat!" he yelled. "I have sick people in the hills that I'm taking care of!" In anger, he kicked out Greg's windshield and threw Greg's car keys over the side of the road into a river.

Then, on Mother's Day, Jeff hoped to come to dinner. He was devastated that he broke Greg's windshield and wanted to pay for it. Sadly, he wasn't allowed to join us. Jeff—the one who had been concerned about Eli being left out the year before—was left out.

In the summer of 2007, I went to Jeff's camp with him to get his earthly belongings which fit in a big plastic bag. He was preparing to leave the hills and move back home. A quiet breeze rustled the trees. The moon was out. A coyote howled as Jeff told me, "I have a pet rat. I don't mind waking up from my sleep to find it chewing on my beard. But one night, I felt something crawling on my face in my sleep and I swatted it without realizing it was my rat. He bit me on the nose. I feel really bad. He is my friend! I also had a pet mouse. One morning I saw that it had fallen into my water cup and drowned. I felt real sad."

A few days after Jeff moved home, we were looking at tools in Harbor Freight. When we stepped out of the store we saw smoke rising from the hills where he had lived only days before. We drove straight there. Jeff ran off barefoot into the hills to be sure all the homeless people were out. Jeff was gone for a long time as the flames spread.

The firemen arrived and drove their truck up an access road. Fireball explosions burst at the sides of their truck— probably from containers of fuel stashed in the bushes. All the firemen except the driver jumped off the truck and backed away in panic, motioning for the driver to get out. The driver backed away from the flames as onlookers and I held our breath, hoping the fire truck wouldn't explode. Jeff still hadn't returned.

After a long wait, Jeff ran up to me and asked for my cell phone. He called the people whose camps he couldn't get to. After finding out that they were safe, Jeff laughed, "When I came out, a fireman yelled at me, 'Don't go in there!' He didn't know I already had!" Then, Jeff got a serious look on his face and said, "I could have gotten killed, but I saw a way to get to the camps and ran in without thinking."

As we left, two policemen saw Jeff and asked him about several homeless persons by name. Jeff accounted for each person.

Jeff and I drove away from the burning hill and saw 60-year-old Mary sitting on some grass on a corner. She had been collecting recyclables out of trash cans when she saw the hills—and her camp—ablaze. As we spoke, I sat down beside her. Mary's eyes were clear and brilliantly blue. She was trim and young looking for 60-years-old. Now, everything she owned was burned up.

"I'll start over again," she said, "As I have done many times before." Then she told me that once when she was drunk Jeff had carried her to safety when someone tried to attack her. She's one of many women who've told me they were rescued from attack by Jeff.

I remember hearing about Charlie, an old homeless man who got beaten so badly that he couldn't walk. When no one was looking, Jeff carried Charlie down the hill to safety before his attackers returned to finish him off. When Charlie got out of the hospital, he camped under the bridge. Jeff brought him food and beer to ease his pain.

My brother-in-law said that Jeff's mission in life might be to live with the homeless.

That summer, after Jeff moved home from his camp, we took in foreign exchange students from Finland, Russia, Denmark and Spain. I volunteered to house them at the last minute due to an emergency even though Tim's wedding was about to take place.

Jeff was by my side picking the students up at the airport. There had been a long delay. Jeff had stayed awake all night, waiting for their flight while I slept in the van. In the weeks that followed, Jeff drove the students to their school every day and on shopping excursions as well. It was wonderful to see Jeff brilliantly sober and radiant at his twin brother's wedding celebration. Then, Tim went on his honeymoon, the students left, and Jeff went back to the hills.

In December 2007, Jeff was living behind an industrial center on Easy Street. There was a large gate and a dry waterfall leading down to the homeless camps.

Jeff invited me to see his camp. He met me at the rock waterfall with a big grin, and then led me down to a trail through the woods. The smell wasn't fresh because debris had settled in parts of the river bed. Then we came to an island formed by the river splitting in two. The water was low enough that I could step on rocks to get to Jeff's island. There were two tents there.

One belonged to a girl named Amy. She had flags, a mirror, an oriental rug at the entrance to her tent, and a clothesline. Jeff's camp was at the other end of the island. It had fire pits, cooking utensils and several trash bags stacked up under a tree. It was clean like his camp had been under the bridge years ago when he worked at Indiana Bones Temple of Groom.

Amy told me that she liked camping by Jeff for protection. A very pretty girl, and an alcoholic, she had been saved by Jeff from lustful men on many occasions.

"Further up the river," Jeff said, "There's a swimming hole I made, with a whirlpool in it. It has terraced steps leading to it that I dug myself. And right over there I have a higher camp for when heavy rains are predicted," he added, pointing to a hill. Then he said, "Once, when it was raining, there was a man down here on this island who couldn't speak English. He was screaming for help as the rivers rose up his legs. He didn't know how to swim. I knew the high and low spots in the river so I was able to carry the man safely across."

One night, I got a call from Amy. "Jeff needs a ride to the hospital," she said. I drove to the gate behind the industrial facility and met Amy, and a big African American man named Jon-Jon who was carrying Jeff. They lifted Jeff into my van and Amy held cloths against the wounds on his face and the back of his head.

"What happened?" I asked, as we drove to the hospital.

Amy said, "There were bloodcurdling screams coming from across the river and Jeff went to see what it was. But before he got to where the screams came from he was pelted by rocks, bloodying his face. He turned away and was crossing the river when a boulder hit the back of his head causing the nastiest gash! He didn't lose consciousness until he made it back to our camp and told us what happened. That's when Jon-Jon and I tried to stop the bleeding and couldn't."

Amy waited up all night with me. The next day, Jeff was released from the hospital with stitches in his wounds.

Not long after, Amy moved to Las Vegas. Jeff and I visited her on one of our trips to Utah. Her friends honored Jeff and me with a big Barbeque feast. Amy was drinking less, and mentally sound. Back in California, she had been tormented by voices that followed her around. She'd shout to the voices, "Go Away! Leave me Alone!"

Jeff had a friend in Simi Valley named Lorin. She had come to visit him in Utah in 2005. Jeff had paid for her bus ticket. When she arrived, she looked distant and frail. Still, Jeff had tried to show her a good time. He drove her to the Grand Canyon, taking off from work at the Steel Mill. Yet afterward, Jeff told me, "I drove her all the way there, a four-hour-round-trip, and when we got there, she didn't even want to get out of the car."

Back in California, a few years passed, and Jeff started dating Lorin again. After spending a few months in a sober home, Lorin was warm and hospitable. "I'd marry her," Jeff told me, "but she can't have any kids, and I want to have children."

Lorin kept dropping out of rehabs. Jeff and I attempted to help her, to no avail. About that time, Jeff was working a job with a party company where he assembled jolly bouncers—the inflatable houses that children jump in at parties. Jeff was living at home.

Jeff was stressed while dating Lorin and dealing with his boss who was overworking him. Lorin visited our home once, and appeared to be a ghost of a person—not really there. Then, Jeff started acting strange after being around her. So I forbade Jeff from having contact with her while he lived under our roof.

Eventually, Jeff moved out. Then, one day, Jeff came home with a scary look on his face and asked to come inside to use our phone. He wanted to call Lorin. I wouldn't let him, so he kicked out the window with his bare foot, reached in, and got the phone. The police came and Jeff quickly tried to down some vodka he had stashed in his pocket. It splashed all over his face as they began to handcuff him. Then he went to jail.

When Jeff got out of jail, he and Lorin broke up. He took the vehicle he'd been living in—a 1989 yellow Datsun motor home—and parked it in our driveway. He dismantled it all over our lawn while Greg and I were gone: flooring, cupboards, paneling, stove, and countless vehicle pieces. Then he disappeared and didn't come back for weeks. While he was gone, we picked up the pieces, put them in the vehicle, and had it towed.

A few months later, I took Jeff grocery shopping. He bought milk and other items. Then we headed for Jack in the Box. On the way, Jeff pulled a vodka bottle out of his backpack and gulped down Vodka with his milk. I pulled into the restaurant parking lot, parked my van, ran inside ahead of Jeff, gave the cashier some money, and told her to give the 6 ½ foot tall man with a beard and ponytail whatever he wanted. Then I passed Jeff coming into the restaurant on my way out. I got to my van, removed Jeff's vodka, backpack, and groceries, and left.

After I got home, my phone rang. It was Jeff with a concerned voice, "Mom, are you ok? I was worried about you when you didn't come back."

CHAPTER SEVEN

Jeff told me, "My friends say I should get on disability. But I'm not retarded!" Greg and I observed that Jeff was happiest while he was working. Work put him in a good mood. Substance abuse was his biggest problem.

About that time, my van broke down. None of the mechanics in town were able to fix it so I sold it to Jeff. He fixed it and sold it back for a higher price. Then he used the money to buy a cute white Volvo. It had belonged to a mechanic who passed away. The mechanic's family was happy to sell it to Jeff, who appreciated the sentimental car. It had a pen light on an electric cord which Jeff loved using for maps at night. Like all of Jeff's cars it was at least 20-years-old—the way Jeff liked them.

Shortly after, some strange people came to our house. There was something eerie about them. They were absent—like bodies without real persons inside. Then Jeff disappeared with them, only to return a few days later with that same vacant expression on his face too. He walked in circles around our house day and night. I didn't let him in. It seemed like the man in my son's body wasn't really my son. Nobody spoke to him as he circled our house and knocked on the door in the middle of the night.

The next thing we knew, Jeff had spread pieces of his white Volvo all over our front yard—the glove box, steering wheel, seats, carpeting, dashboard, battery, radiator and more. He cut the wires inside the engine into pieces. He placed its tires at the side of the house to make chairs to sit on.

Later, I stood beside Jeff as we watched a tow truck take away what had once been a nice car—and all the pieces from it. I didn't know what to say. Jeff wouldn't acknowledge that his loss was due to drugs.

I began requiring Jeff to attend an AA meeting for every night that he slept under our roof. He also set an appointment for counseling with our angelic friend and counselor Laura Denke. Greg and I took him to see our counselor Laura. With tears in her eyes, she said she was deeply touched by what a good-hearted person Jeff was. She set up interviews for Jeff at drug rehabs. Greg took off from work to take Jeff to the appointments. There was one ritzy rehab with a swimming pool, antique furniture, a cook who used to cook for the Prince of Denmark, and clients who took cruises when they were not in rehab. There was the rescue mission in Oxnard. There was River Community—a dual diagnosis rehab for persons with mental disabilities and addictions. All of the rehabs refused Jeff or didn't seem right for him—except for River Community.

River Community is located in the Los Angeles National Forest. After passing rivers, dams and lakes we arrived in the mountain retreat for his interview. After the interview, we complied with all of their requirements—we took Jeff to see a psychiatrist twice and put him on medication. The psychiatrist had suggested Jeff go straight to the rehab, but River Community required he be on medication for two weeks before entering their program.

After two weeks, Jeff was only worse. Yet he had fulfilled the requirements—including getting signed up for disability. The rehab would only take clients if they were on disability.

When we took Jeff with packed bags to the intake interview, we expected him to get help. However, after the interview they refused him. "He doesn't want to recover," the person in charge said.

Soon, Jeff's monthly disability checks were coming to me as his payee. I paid off his old medical bills and court fines. It took me months to do so and it was no small headache. But I was determined to open up a debt-free future for Jeff. However, he was not happy. He wanted drug money. I told him this money was for responsible things. At one point, Jeff found a room to rent which I paid for with his disability money. But he left the room, never to return, after staying only one night. The month's rent was lost.

Around the same time, Greg got a restraining order to keep Jeff from coming within 50 feet of our house—due to his frightening behavior. As Jeff's payee, I met him across the street from our home, or at a store, and tried to help him get healthy things.

I marvel that Greg and I stayed close through all of this. I didn't want a restraining order. We took different approaches. Yet one thing we had in common was our mutual love for Jeff.

Greg handled his concern for Jeff in a quiet way. From the time Jeff turned twelve-years-old, Greg has fasted every Sunday from food and water to exercise his faith on Jeff's behalf.

One day, I drove by the street where Lorin lived with her mother. I felt powerfully drawn toward Lorin's mother—who had become my friend. She used to give me fresh homemade bread and compliment me on what a fine son I had before Jeff and Lorin broke up.

I pulled over at the side of the road, considering a visit to Lorin's mother to thank her for the homemade bread she used to send. For several minutes I sat there in my van. Finally, I decided not to visit her that day because I was tired. I went home and took a nap instead. "Another day," I said. "Another day I'll tell Lorin's mother I appreciate her—when I'm not so tired."

That day was the day Lorin stabbed her mother to death. I took it hard when I found out. For weeks I had insomnia, pangs of despair, and wondered if I could have stopped the murder if I hadn't forgone my visit that day. It would have been about the time of the murder that I was parked at the side of the road contemplating whether I should visit her.

Jeff hadn't seen Lorin for a year. When I told him about her mother's death, he said nothing. It was hard for me to see what he felt beneath his silence.

News of what happened to Lorin's mother sent fear through my children and Greg concerning my welfare. It wasn't until Jeff got on Disability that the fear of being hurt by him became real to me too.

About that time, I grew too fatigued to meet Jeff across the street, take him shopping, and check his receipts. Before getting disability pay, Jeff had earned money from odd jobs and recycling cans. He bought his own phone with money he earned. I remember his big smile as he showed me a phone which he purchased from recycling cans.

Yet, when he was on disability, and I bought him phones with the government money, he'd break them every time. He threw phones against rocks or trees, or he'd stomp on them. He threw some in the river. On a few occasions, his phones were returned to him after people heard them ringing under the water. He once told me, with a laugh, "Phones are hard to break!"

No good came out of helping Jeff get disability assistance—except for paying medical bills and debts—which Jeff cared little about. There was no change in his life except for more drug use.

Out of sheer exhaustion, I started giving Jeff small amounts of disability money. The first time I gave Jeff money, in 2008, I hoped and prayed he'd use it wisely. However, he returned too quickly for more.

At that time, I had a rescue horse named Cinnamon Candy which was boarded on Leads Street, a mile from our home. I walked there every day and spent most of my time there. I made the horse boarding place my hangout. Jeff met me there, where I had time to visit, relaxing in comfort on bales of hay. I hoped Jeff would use his magic touch on my rescue horse. However, all he wanted was money. Strange friends started coming with him. The more his friends were around the quicker he ran out of money. I grew more and more frightened of his visits. I realized there was no place for me to run to for help if I was in harm's way.

One day Jeff came alone and I told him that I had no money as he watched me lead my horse out to the arena. Earlier, I had fastened her new soft sheepskin saddle, making the cinch firm as I did with hard saddles. Now, with Jeff by my side, I offered to let him ride her. He got on Candy's back as she stood still. The instant he sat on her she went crazy. Jeff quickly got off her back, saying, "Something's wrong."

I hadn't realized that I had cinched the soft saddle too tight for her to bear weight without injury. Later that night, I got a call. It was the owner of the horse boarding place. Candy had thrown herself onto the ground convulsing in pain, and had torn up the fencing and dirt in her stable.

"Colic," the property owner said.

I stayed with Candy day and night. She stopped eating and drinking. The vet treated her for colic, to no avail. I walked her around the arena where we had many happy memories. I spoke lovingly to her. I brushed and braided her tail and mane, with a lantern on the fence post at night, coaxing her up when she laid down.

The next morning, the vet told me to buy a special bran mash for her to eat. I bought the mash and when I returned, Candy was lying down in the pasture. I quickly made the gruel and headed out to her with it. She was dead. I looked away from the flies landing on her glossed over eyes and imagined her spirit trotting through the clouds. She was no longer in pain.

I stayed with her body, arranging for a horse burial truck to come. Jeff walked up as they laid her body in the back of the truck. But it wasn't Jeff. He looked like a wild man and I was scared. He wanted money, but I said, "Sorry," and hopped into the truck carrying Candy's body. Then I said to the driver, "Let's get out of here." The driver dropped me off at my home—a safe place because of the restraining order.

Later, Jeff came to his sister Christy and Steve's wedding. He sat next to his sister Butterfly who was pregnant with twins. He was clean, sober, and handsome.

We bought Jeff a plane ticket to Hawaii for his brother Eli's wedding. However, Jeff called right before our drive to the airport to say he wasn't feeling well enough to come.

The next week, tears rolled down Eli's checks as he made his vows with his wife on the shore of an aqua sea. It was one of the most beautiful moments of my life, saddened only by the fact that all of our family wasn't there.

Right before Halloween 2008, torrential rains were predicted. Jeff worked hard on making his new friend Leta's camp high and dry. When the rains came all of the camps were flooded and many were washed away—except for Leta's. Her camp was the only one in the west hills that survived.

I had been trying to buy Jeff healthy things, but not give him money. Matt, my buff teenager coached me to say, "No," when Jeff asked for cash.

Then the night of the Halloween Festival came. I picked up the phone and called Jeff, "They're having a harvest dinner at church tonight. Would you like to come?"

"Ahh, I'd like to see my family and I'm hungry," he said.

"I can pick you up at the Décor Store," I suggested.

Jeff agreed. I headed for the store near Jeff's hill. The last time I had met him there, hoping to take him out for lunch, I realized after he got into my van that he was stoned. I drove in circles around the parking lot a few times, then stopped and opened the door to let him out. He got out and walked off in a daze. I hoped this time would be better.

When I arrived, Jeff didn't look right. I thought he was only tired from moving camps to higher ground to prepare for the next storm. I let him into my van and drove onto the freeway. I started some small talk, "Matt had no Halloween costume, so he decided to dress up as a girl. He borrowed one of my dresses and some jewelry—"

Suddenly Jeff began cussing, something he never does when he's sober. Frightened, I drove on in silence, fearful that anything I said might agitate him. The thought passed through my mind that he could take the steering wheel and yank our car out of control at any second. I silently prayed to be able to get off the freeway safely.

I took the freeway off-ramp, rounded a corner, and stopped at my friend Debbie's house. Jeff and I had a routine of going to Debbie's before our outings. I used to baby-sit Debbie when I was a teenager. Now she was a recovered alcoholic. She knew that Jeff wasn't allowed in our house. She let Jeff take showers at her house.

"Here are clean clothes, shampoo and soap," I said to Jeff, hoping he'd switch back to his natural self again. He set the clothes on the dashboard and sat there in silence.

After waiting a long time, he said, "I don't want to clean up."

It was then that I lost hope of him going to the church dinner. He sat in my van with a blank stare. My intuition warned me that I was in danger. "I'm going to drive you back to the hills," I announced as I slowly pulled out of Debbie's driveway and eased myself back into traffic.

"I don't want to go back to the hills yet!" Jeff protested. "I've been up for two nights moving my friend's camp to higher ground and I'm tired! I want something to eat! And I want to see my family!"

"I'll drive home and get something for you to eat. Then I'll take you back to the hills," I replied. I drove to our home, parked the van across the street, and went inside to get some food.

Shortly, I got back in the van and handed Jeff a freshly baked loaf of bread and a bottle of salsa. As I slowly drove down the street, I sensed an impending explosion. I prayed, but with little faith, that it would be safe to drive with Jeff in my car.

Suddenly, Jeff cussed and thrust the open bottle of salsa into the van door, splattering gooey green sauce all over the dashboard, windshield and ceiling.

I pulled over and stopped the van, demanding, "You need to get out of my car! You're scaring me!"

Jeff replied, "This is my van—not yours! It's my van!"

I wondered what made him say that. Was it the memory of him fixing my van when the professional mechanics couldn't fix it? I had paid him. The van wasn't his.

"It's my van!" Jeff shouted again, angry. I took my keys out of the ignition, opened my door and stepped out. I walked over to a juniper tree a few yards away and dialed 911. I knew I couldn't drive him back to the hills without risking an accident.

Within five minutes, three police cruisers arrived. They flashed their headlights into my van. Jeff continued eating the bread and salsa. Using a loudspeaker, the officers ordered him to get out of the van. He wouldn't budge.

I had feared for myself, but now I feared for Jeff. I recalled that a mentally ill man down the street had barricaded himself in a house and refused to leave.

After a long standoff, he was shot and killed. I didn't want the same thing to happen to Jeff.

The police waited for Jeff to obey their order, while he just sat there eating.

A lot of time passed. An officer walked up to me.

"Can you tell me what happened?" he asked.

I explained Jeff's behavior. I tried to protect Jeff by saying that he was autistic—although he'd never been scientifically diagnosed. Then I added that he was addicted to Crystal Meth.

The officer replied, "He may be autistic. But this behavior is not from autism. It's from drugs." Then he stood by me as if to protect me, and I silently prayed, *God, help Jeff and the police.*

The next time that the police ordered Jeff to get out of the van, the vehicle started shaking. At that moment some neighborhood children rounded the corner. With wide eyes, the children froze on the sidewalk— watching the van heave and shake as Jeff kicked the windshield from the inside of the car. He kept kicking the windshield over and over again as we watched in shock.

When the window was bulging way out, Jeff stopped kicking. He quietly shoved away the crumbling windshield and climbed out of the opening where the window had been. He then perched himself on top of the van's dashboard, hunched down low at first. Then, he eased his body up to its full height—looming high above the roof. No one made a sound.

The wind stirred Jeff's black trench coat. Unbuttoned, it began flapping wildly. His long hair blew in every direction. I looked at his face peering down at us as he towered above us in the air. For a moment, he reminded me of the Hulk creature which he used to watch in cartoons.

The children, the police, and I looked at Jeff, as if frozen in time. Then, all of a sudden, Jeff sprung from the dashboard onto the street. Seeing him hit the ground, the neighborhood children screamed and ran away. Jeff squatted low on the asphalt, turning his head to the left and to the right. I held my breath. A myriad of thoughts passed through my mind: *Did he hurt himself jumping down? Was he going to charge the police? Would they shoot?*

No one moved. Then, slowly, Jeff prostrated himself face-down on the asphalt and put his hands behind his back. Perhaps he'd learned from previous arrests that it only makes things worse to resist.

In January 2009 Jeff got out of jail for kicking out my windshield. He went to Kentucky to visit his sister Butterfly's family. Butterfly hoped Jeff would start a new life there.

During an ice storm, Jeff helped Butterfly and her four small children survive while Dragonfly—a paramedic—was off rescuing people from injury who had been trapped in the freezing cold by accidents or fallen trees. Jeff and the girls were without electricity and running water. Jeff kept one room of their house heated with a kerosene heater. In that room, Jeff melted ice into water and cooked for Butterfly and her four daughters on a propane stove.

Jeff stayed in Kentucky after the storm and Butterfly became his payee. Yet too soon after, Jeff decided to return to California and took a flight home. Then, Butterfly mailed the rest of Jeff's money which she didn't use for food back to the government, telling me it's dangerous and a very bad idea to be his payee.

After Butterfly quit being Jeff's payee, Jeff got another at Simi Valley's Samaritan Center who helped him use his disability money to buy a little economy car—a blue one. He got it registered and insured and kept his license current. One night some women from the hills above his camp came down to him and asked for a ride to the hospital. One of the women was pregnant and had started labor.

Jeff later told me, "I was nervous driving to the hospital. Halfway there they told me to pull over and get out of the car. Then, after the baby was born in the back seat, they called me back to the car to drive them the rest of the way to the hospital." With a look of relief Jeff added, "The mother and baby were fine."

Later, I wrote in my diary on July 11, 2009: "Jeff called from the Wal-Mart pay phone. He used the money he panhandled there to make his call. He asked how the family is doing—asking by name about each brother and sister—and especially about his twin brother's baby. Then I heard nothing from him for over a week. *I wonder if he's alive. My thoughts are drawn out to the universe, past the walls of my home, past the homeless camps in the hills, and up to the sky. I feel connected to heaven. Is Jeff in heaven or on earth? I hope he's on earth. I'll be glad to hear he's still alive.*

Like wolves, Jeff's 'friends' packed around him when he got his disability pay. He was continually tracked down by strange friends asking for money. Sometimes his disability money would disappear and Jeff wouldn't know who took it.

Several of Jeff's friends have died. One nice guy was found in a dumpster. One guy, who had recovered from drug addiction, was happy to see his children again, but died shortly after of an overdose.

My family went to a housewarming for Jeff's brother. Jeff was not invited. I missed Jeff. When he's around, he takes extra time to look at family photo albums. To Jeff, family is everything—our family, and the homeless people who he also calls "family." Later, to my delight, Matt invited Jeff to his birthday dinner at a restaurant.

As a child, Jeff always tested out in school at 5% for social skills. With his disability pay attracting swarms of people, Jeff couldn't resist the pressure. He couldn't even manage keeping a car. His blue economy car was about to be towed and he asked me to help him clean it out. There I found the tiny oxygen mask that the medical team had brought to his car after the baby was born. I saved it as a keepsake of when a baby was born in Jeff's car.

After that car, Jeff got another car without tags. He kept it off-road until his hand got cut while protecting someone in a fight. In his emergency he drove his car to a doctor. Then, while he was getting stitches on his hand in the doctor's office, the car was impounded. Jeff told me, "It had all my tools in it which were worth lots of money." Other cars he bought with his disability money were impounded too.

Later, Jeff's arrest for possession of a controlled substance—and his court order to go to Freedom House—led us back to the harbor.

PART THREE

CHAPTER EIGHT

Channel Islands Harbor
February 2010

I was living in our sailboat. Jeff was living in our van on the shore nearby. The boat rocked when Jeff jumped aboard. "I'll call Freedom House to see if they have an opening after breakfast," he said.

Jeff finished two bowls of oatmeal and called the sober house. After the call, he said, "Freedom House doesn't have an opening yet. I'll call back tomorrow. I have a few dollars, so I'm taking a walk."

He wandered off in the direction of the liquor store. He didn't smell good, his long blond hair was knotted, and his clothing was torn. I hoped his stay at Freedom House would turn his life around.

I heard a plop in the water and turned to see a baby seal. I picked up some lunch meat and held it over the water. The seal repeatedly came close to my hand, and then darted away. Staying with Jeff at the harbor had delights like this which I loved.

Jeff returned and walked past our boat to the end of the dock. I saw no alcohol.

Moments later, I sat down beside Jeff, our feet dangling above the water as we watched egrets and ducks. A seagull squalled. "I have no crackers to feed you," I told the seagull.

"Ahh! We could give him some beer," Jeff laughed. Then he began telling half-finished stories, "Two knives braised past me at the same time from opposite directions—one across my stomach and one across my back. I was trying to stop a fight between two friends." Jeff said.

He began mumbling. I noticed his blistered toes and bruised fingers. He was missing a few fingernails. He reminded me of the derelicts that Greg and I used to drive past when we visited Venice Beach. I gave my coat to one of them and the elderly stranger who had been shivering put it on while mumbling unintelligently. I looked back at Jeff, whose mumbling had fallen silent. I prayed he'd not stay this way.

The hours passed, sitting on the dock beside Jeff. Then, I stood up and announced, "It's time to fix lunch." I took a few steps, glanced back, and saw a brown-bagged bottle sticking out of Jeff's coat pocket.

I caught a whiff of liquor in the air and wondered how he'd taken a swig and replaced the bottle so quickly. "Remember the time you flushed your drugs down the toilet and vowed to live clean? It would be nice if you'd do the same again with this liquor," I said.

I went to the harbor restroom to wash my hands for lunch. When I came out, Jeff was sitting on a patch of grass beside the restroom, staring off into space.

I sat down beside him. He seemed unaware of my presence. I saw his coat pocket hanging open, reached into his pocket, took out the bottle of malt liquor from the brown bag, walked back into the restroom, flushed it down the toilet, and returned to Jeff. There he sat, oblivious, with an empty brown bag in his pocket. I walked to my van to get lunch at the same moment that three fishermen walked by and passed Jeff. Suddenly, Jeff noticed his bottle was gone. He ran up to the fishermen asking, "Hey! Did one of you take my bottle?" They denied taking it. Dejected, Jeff walked over to me. I held up a bag of potatoes and asked, "What would you like for lunch?"

Jeff blurted out, "Someone took my bottle! I saw them walk away with it but when I asked them for it, they said they didn't take it!" I handed Jeff a box of food to carry, and together we went to our boat where Jeff gulped down potatoes, broccoli, cheese, two hard-boiled eggs, a tuna fish sandwich, and some peppercorns—which he popped into his mouth whole, like candy. Satisfied, he went back to the van alone.

I washed the dishes and returned to the van. There I saw Jeff bent over, picking something up from off the ground.

"What are you doing?" I asked.

"Ahh, I'm just picking up glass."

How nice, I thought to myself. *Someone must have broken a bottle and Jeff's beautifying the parking lot.*

Moments later, I got in the driver's seat. Jeff sat in the passenger seat with our dog on his lap. I drove to the sandy shore, and we watched the waves in silence. Jeff's baby brother, 16-year-old Matt called my cell phone. Matt had broken his collarbone while skiing a few days earlier. He wanted to let me know he was managing well without me. Before coming to the harbor I'd waited on Matt, bringing him food during his painful recovery and watching the "Lord of the Rings" trilogy.

"I drove to school all by myself using one hand," Matt proudly announced. I felt relieved that both Matt and Jeff didn't need me at the same time. Matt's call ended, and Jeff suggested we go to the L-shaped pier up the road.

I remembered the water spray on Greg's and my faces as we took a romantic walk on that pier. I knew exactly how to get there. I started the van's engine and in no time we parked at the pier. I opened my van door and said, "Stretch your legs Jonny!" Jonny took off like a bullet.

Jeff and I watched Jonny run on the sand. A breeze picked up as the sun dipped behind a cloud. I put on my sweater. Yet I began to shiver in the cold. I closed the windows. Still, cold air was coming in. I looked around for an open window that I had missed. Suddenly, I saw it—a side window was missing. The soft rubber lining was intact, but the entire plate of glass was gone. A flash of memory reminded me of Jeff picking up glass earlier. I looked at Jeff.

Jeff bowed his head in shame and said, "I broke the window because I was mad that someone took my drink."

I thought of calling the police. But I didn't feel frightened, I recalled the time that I threw a dinner plate through our dining room window in anger. My husband Greg didn't call the police on me. I had been medicated then for mental illness and the medications tended to make me violent.

The sun came out from behind the clouds and the sea sparkled again. Relentless breakers crashed on the sand, reminding me of the countless windows Jeff broke, which can be replaced. It was Jeff's life that I feared losing the most.

Jeff looked up, his eyes following Jonny who was zig-zagging up and down the shore, taking in the smells.

"Let's go," Jeff said.

I called Jonny. He came running back into our van and we drove up the road. "I think I'm going to throw up because I haven't had any beer today," Jeff said.

I pulled into an empty lot with dry bushes and Jeff relieved himself.

I remembered when I went through withdrawal from my psychiatric medications. I threw up like never before, and couldn't sleep for 48 hours. It was the worst pain I ever had—even worse than having a baby. Yet things got better after a few days.

Jeff got back in the van after throwing up. I then drove to a store to buy tape and plastic for the broken window. When I returned to the van, Jeff said, "The Rescue Mission is up the road." We drove to the mission and parked.

Suddenly Jeff blurted out, "We can't leave Jonny in the van or he'll jump out the window! I don't want to eat at the Mission anymore!" he yelled, slamming his fist into the windshield. I was relieved when I saw that the window hadn't broken. Still, Jeff insisted we not go in the mission for dinner. So I prayed out loud, *God, what shall I do? It would be nice to go in the mission, but Jeff doesn't want to.* Suddenly, an idea popped into my head: *Tie Jonny's leash to the steering wheel.* I tied Jonny's leash.

"I said, I don't want to eat," Jeff reminded me, as I fished shoes out of the clothing bag that I kept for him in my car. I handed him shoes, ignoring his protest, and got out of my van.

At that moment, a man came up to me and said, "A train will be coming by. You need to move your van." Another man overheard us and moved his car forward so that I could move my van further from the tracks. Jeff began putting on his shoes.

"You must be new here," a hunched back man said as he joined us on our way to the mission door. "My name is David. I like your van. I once had one like it, but my dad sold it while I was in a coma." Then, David looked at Jeff and said, "You should appreciate your parents. My mom and dad passed away and I miss them."

In the mission we sat beside David as plates of ham, mashed potatoes, gravy, and vegetables were served. Jeff ate all of his dinner and mine too. It looked and smelled delicious. Yet I didn't touch the food because I was fasting dinner, in hopes that my fast would make a statement to God that I wanted Him to help my son.

The next day, at the harbor, Jeff said, "I'm worried about Bobby."

"Why?" I asked. My thoughts drifted to the last time I'd seen Bobby.

Last December when Jeff walked out of Freedom House, he went back to the hills. Then, he called me from a pay phone at Wal-Mart. "Mom, will you take me back to Freedom House?" he asked. "If they don't have an opening, we could wait on the boat." I went to Wal-Mart to pick him up. There I saw Bridget and Bobby, panhandling with a dog.

I rolled down my window to ask, "Where's Jeff?"

Bobby ran up to my window, "Look! We made over a hundred dollars! People are really nice at Christmas time." Then he answered my question, "Jeff is in front of the store."

I approached the store and let Jeff into my van. He was happy to see me. I wondered if he was stable enough to not break another window. In order to feel safe, I tried a tactic that I had used before.

"Mind if I read a page to you from El Libro?" I asked. The Spanish words "El Libro" translate to English as "The Book." "El Libro" is a nickname I use for a book of scripture—a testament of God's hope for people like Jeff and me.

I remembered that before we got the restraining order, sometimes Jeff came down from the hills to our house while on Meth. He'd have an unusual gait, a hard set jaw and a strange, hard stare on his face. It sent eerie chills up my spine. Once when Jeff walked up like a zombie from hell, I held up El Libro and said, "We need to read a few verses before I let you in." He cussed and ran back to the hills. A few days later, he returned and let me read as he lay down. As I read, his body jerked back and forth as if demons were leaving him. Then he settled into a peaceful sleep. That was years ago.

In the Wal-Mart parking lot, shoppers walked by, and Jeff replied, "I don't mind if you read."

I opened the book and began to read, *They buried their swords in the ground and vowed to never shed blood again. Then, their enemies came with their swords glimmering in the sun. The men without swords knelt down and prayed, saying, "It's better we let ourselves be slain because we are prepared to meet God, than to take the life of a brother who was unprepared to die."*

I finished reading, and Jeff sat there calmly. He had passed the test by listening without cussing. I took a deep breath and let out a sigh of relief. I started the engine and began our trip to Freedom House. As we approached the parking lot exit, Bridget, Bobby and their dog stopped us. "Will you drop us off at the bridge?" Bobby asked.

I let them into my van, and Bobby began flirting. "Jeff, your Mom's hot for having had seven kids. If your dad wants to trade Bridget for her, I'm game."

Jeff said to Bobby, "Shut up."

The memory of last December finished swimming in my head.

I realized that Jeff hadn't answered my question about Bobby as we sat beside the harbor. "Why? Why are you worried about Bobby?" I asked.

"Bobby might be dead," Jeff said.

I waited for Jeff to say more. After a long silence I gently probed again, "Why do you say Bobby might be dead?"

"There was a fight last week under the bridge. I was holding back two dogs," Jeff said. His brow furrowed in an expression of agony as he spoke. "I couldn't stop the fight because I had to hold the dogs back. If I let them go they would have made things worse." Jeff looked down and shrugged with a helpless look. "Last I saw Bobby his face was bashed in by a rock and he wasn't moving."

My soul sunk, knowing that it could have been Jeff. I recalled a time that Jeff came home with a bandaged hand after stopping his drunk friends from killing each other. They had picked up a machete and an ax by the campfire and lunged at each other. "I didn't feel myself getting cut," Jeff had told me. "I didn't notice the blood until the fight was over. Then, while I was sewing stitches in my hand, the two guys acted like nothing had happened, and joked about the whole thing, slapping each other on the back."

Countless times I have glanced toward the hills and wondered if Jeff was still alive. A gloom settled over us as we sat in silence. Then I said, "I read somewhere that death only has an ugly mask. If we knew what lay beyond, we would run, run, run and leap into eternity." Jeff listened and bowed his head as I said a prayer for Bobby—in case he was still alive, that he'd recover. And if he passed, that he would be at peace.

Jeff crawled into the bed in the back of my van and took a nap.

Later, I got to thinking that Jeff and I could read El Libro in eight days if we read about 60 pages a day. I said to myself: *Today is February 10th. By February 18th—next Thursday—we'll be done!* The thought gave me something positive to hold onto while waiting for Freedom House to have an opening.

When Jeff awoke, I noticed his clear blue eyes. They looked compassionate, the way I picture Jesus' eyes to look. Sunlight streamed through an opening in the clouds and a hush fell over the harbor. Later, Jeff ate the sandwiches I gave him and went back to sleep.

The stars came out in the night sky. Both Jeff and I were more tired than hungry. We skipped dinner. The world seemed to stop. I loved the stillness. The quietness. There's a peace about nature that calms the soul.

After staying in bed for 24 hours, Jeff finally got up. He smelt like he hadn't bathed for weeks, but at least he was alive. And at least for one day, sober.

He asked for my phone and called Freedom House to see if they had an opening.

"Not yet. Maybe tomorrow," they said. Then, Jeff stood up, and walked toward the liquor store.

Later he bounced back onto the boat, happy because he'd pan-handled some beer. "Let's go sailing. I'll save my beer until we get back," he said, "And I'll take a shower before we go."

He walked to the restroom to shower. Then I noticed that my long braids had come unraveled. This would be a day for both of us to clean up and start having fun!

Jeff and I cut our sailing trip short. The sea was rough and the waves tossed our boat so high that the propellers barely touched the water. We feared to raise the sails because the fierce gusts of wind could tear them. Before our journey barely began, we returned to dock. Jeff returned to the van and taped plastic over the broken window. Then he ate a few tuna fish sandwiches and lay down on the van's bed as I read El Libro. He popped his can of beer open, tipped it, and then set it down before it reached his lips. "I don't want to drink in front of you," he said. He nestled down in the van bed, listening to me read, like a child searching for meaning.

Jeff and I went to the Rescue Mission for dinner. Standing in line in front of us was Bobby—the friend who Jeff thought was dead.

With delight, we joined a shaky Bobby who was going through withdrawal. I let him borrow my cell phone to call his mother in Florida.

"I've signed up to live at the mission for 6 months," he told his mother. His face was bruised from the fight, yet his eyes shone clear and bright.

The Mission served a good meal. I cleaned my plate by scraping my meat, potatoes, and vegetables onto Jeff's and Bobby's plates. I was fasting.

That evening, Jeff and I took a walk and met two old men. When I mentioned Jeff's wait to get into Freedom house, one of the men got excited and said, "They hold AA meetings on the other side of the harbor at Peninsula Park—it's the building that looks like a lighthouse."

Jeff had noticed that lighthouse-shaped-building before, saying, "I wonder what that building is?"

Shortly, Jeff attended his first recovery meeting at Peninsula Park. I waited outside and spoke to a stranger. He said, "The meeting will help your son. Lots of people come who are still drinking. Yet, after coming regularly, they quit."

After the meeting, Jeff and I finished reading one eighth of El Libro. Jeff folded freshly washed laundry while I translated the words that Jeff didn't know. We both speak broken Spanish—or try to.

The next day, Jeff inspected the boom sheets—the ropes for the sail over the cockpit. It's called the boom, because when it rotates to change direction, it hits you in your head if you don't duck.

We motored to the marina store to purchase new ropes and to look at bilge pumps for draining our boat's water supply. Jeff suggested we put in fresh water. Later, Jeff charged the boat battery while we sat eating potatoes and split pea soup. I started an evening fast on Jeff's behalf, and read the next part of El Libro.

Jeff attended Peninsula Park's recovery meeting for the second time and called Freedom House. No opening. The director was pleased that Jeff was attending meetings and said, "Keep attending those meetings and calling me daily, and at your next court date I'll write a good letter for the judge."

Jeff hung up and walked toward the liquor store.

CHAPTER NINE

At the harbor I write—my diary being my lifeline to sanity.

February 13, 2010: With a sense of impending doom, I sit alone on our boat, waiting for Jeff to come for breakfast. His former payee from the Samaritan Center told me that she'd never seen Jeff sober and that she knew he used the money for drugs—which caused him time and again to end up in the mental hospital after getting paid.

His new payee is his cousin Diane. Hopefully she will be better than his last payee, and not give him any cash. I sent her a message to give his disability money to Freedom House to cover his lodging.

February 14, 2010: I'm tired of living with Jeff, tired of the way the boat and car are getting messy, tired of seeing Jeff drink a beer or two a day, and tired of missing Greg. Jeff's trying to get money from Diane and she will not pick up the phone. He's still going to AA meetings, drinking less than before, and reading El Libro. I won't give up yet.

February 15, 2010, Dawn: Greg visited me last night, and warned me not to get between Jeff and his money—for my safety. Jeff said he's afraid he might hurt somebody if he doesn't get the money. Freedom House still has no opening.

Jeff just bounced onto the boat to cook his breakfast with unusual energy. He asked for my cell phone to call Diane. Fear shot through me in anticipation of Jeff getting mad if Diane won't send him money. Yet I feel I'll be safe for a few more hours because Jeff is due to report his progress in court. For that, he'll stay sober.

Afternoon Diary: Jeff went to court and was given more time to get into the sober house.

Presently, I'm sitting under a tree, a few miles from the Harbor. My dog is sniffing a gopher hole. A few minutes ago, I was driving 50 miles per hour, away from the courthouse toward the Rescue Mission, for lunch. I was enjoying the beauty of the countryside and the fresh air when Jeff asked to use my cell phone. I reluctantly handed him my phone and continued driving.

"Hello," I heard Jeff say, "Is Diane there?"

He listened to a reply and then stuck his arm out the window and threw my phone off into a fallow farm field, yelling, "Every time I call her, she's not there!" Then Jeff said, "I'm sorry. Pull over and I'll find your phone."

Now my van is parked on the dirt, and Jeff is walking back and forth looking through the brush for my phone. I hope he tires himself out. It feels good to rest under this tree, away from my van and the harbor—the places that I'm getting tired of. Freedom House has no opening. We have three days left before we finish reading El Libro.

The sun has moved, taking away my shade. For over an hour Jeff's been searching, and hasn't found my phone. I pray he won't find it. His contorted countenance—while in pursuit of money for buying Crystal Meth—is scaring me.

"Let's go. We'll be late for lunch," Jeff says. He gave up his search.

We had lunch at the Mission with Bobby. He's never looked so good. He quit hitting on me and was pleasantly sober. He says his mind's in a fuzz and he has night sweats that drench him. Yet he's happy with his new life.

Jeff and I drove to Point Hueneme Beach after lunch. There, I parked under a shade tree and read another eighth from El Libro. Jeff listened to me read about opposites:

Freedom versus captivity.
Joy versus misery.
Love versus hate.

I've never noticed before how frequently El Libro mentions hope—even for those in the lowest circumstances. Jeff paid attention to the words I read. With no phone for Jeff to call Diane, his obsession quiets down. He naps in the van while I watch the waves with my dog.

Evening: After another long day I retire. Jeff had only one beer today—not three like yesterday. The difference it makes on my sanity is phenomenal. Last night I dreamt that Jeff was trying to kill me and laid awake until the sun came up. Tonight I feel as peaceful as can be.

Still no opening at Freedom House.

February 16, 2010: Jeff didn't drink today. As a result, he was a good repair man. He replaced the main sheet—the line that controls the main sail. Then we sailed to the oil rig, enjoying a frisky seal that barked "Hello" and dolphins swimming beside us. We read one eighth of El Libro.

At day's end, Jeff searched the roadside again and found my phone. He called Diane. She wired him four hundred dollars. Jeff gave me two hundred dollars to save for him before he walked into the AA meeting.

Now I'm in bed in our boat, and Jeff's gone. With two hundred dollars in his pocket.

I pray God send angels for his protection. I feel comfort.

February 17, 2010, 2 AM: Jeff hasn't come back to our boat. I tell myself, *Don't panic. Trust God.*

A still small voice whispers: *Don't talk to Jeff—except to read El Libro. But shouldn't I insist that Jeff not drink in my presence?* I argue.

The spirit whispers: *Lie Low!*

Jeff jumped inside our boat at the crack of dawn. "I ran halfway across town to meet some friends," he said. I knew he was on Meth.

Jeff and I then read 50 pages from El Libro in the boat's kitchen. At the end of our reading, Jeff read with a deliberate and pained expression. Then, he poured fuel on our boat's stove and lit it with a match. The flame flared up with a whoosh. Nothing exploded or got burned, except my nerves. I'm frightened. Jeff's mind reminds me of the times that he destroyed vehicles by cutting wires and dismantling them while he was on Meth.

Later: For ten hours today, Jeff and I checked alternative rehabs because Freedom House still has no opening.

First, we tried Santa Paula's Joshua House, spending all morning looking for the place. The address had changed and we got lost. We eventually found the place and Jeff had an interview. He was turned away because they required a psychiatric evaluation and their doctor had no openings for over a month.

I drove on, in search of an alternative doctor who could evaluate Jeff. Jeff rocked back and forth in the passenger seat as if in a fog. Finally, we found a doctor. Her office was a few blocks away from Freedom House. We'd noticed it before—a bright bungalow with a rainbow colored sign.

Jeff and I entered her waiting room and noticed boxes of supplies, a golden retriever with a bandana around her neck, and a coffee percolator. It gave off a cozy smell. A sign on the table read, "Help Yourself."

I spoke to the receptionist and sensed that this medical facility was different in a good way. The doctor, dressed in a bright yellow dress, came out of a hall and sat down on a chair in the waiting room next to me. When we finished speaking, I breathed a sigh of relief and called Joshua House. "You told me Jeff needed a doctor's evaluation," I said to the director. "I found a doctor who has time to evaluate him."

The director of Joshua House refused, saying, "The evaluation has to be from a psychiatric doctor, not a regular doctor."

Now, here we are at sunset, and I'm afraid Jeff might destroy my boat by playing with fire—or my van by cutting its wires. I've checked us into a Motel—a small room where I can keep an eye on him. I'll sleep by the door with my shoes on, ready to run in case Jeff becomes agitated. I checked out the surrounding area and found several escape routes where I can hide or get help. Yet something whispers to my heart: *Don't worry*.

We have more appointments scheduled for tomorrow at drug rehabs, and we're due to finish reading El Libro tonight.

Almost Midnight: Jeff's been awake for 40 hours. I read from El Libro to him. As I read, he made drawings in a tablet of animals, including our dog Jonny. Nothing scary or violent. After finishing El Libro, I hummed lullabies. Finally, he fell asleep.

February 18, 2010, Morning: Jeff is in the bathroom getting dressed for interviews at rehabs. I'm amazed at the peace I feel. We finished reading El Libro.

I filled his vodka bottle halfway up with water, while he was in the bathroom. When he came out and drank from it he didn't even notice.

Afternoon: Jeff interviewed at Khepler House, after which the interviewer said to me, "During our interview, your son pulled out a vodka bottle and began drinking it! That is disrespectful!" Jeff grinned. He wasn't accepted at that rehab.

Next Jeff interviewed at Vista Del Mar Psychiatric Hospital. He was drunk. The interviewer asked Jeff, "Do you hear voices? Do you want to hurt yourself?"

Jeff answered, "No," and reached into his pocket and patted his bottle.

Then the interviewer turned to me and said, "You seem stressed. Have you considered counseling?"

I was speechless. I've had counseling with more counselors and for more years than I can count. Yet there are some things that counseling can't remove: Heartbreak. Disappointment. Love. Exhaustion from just hanging on.

"Distress is unavoidable," I replied.

"His condition's not critical enough, the interviewer said. "We can't accept him."

Moments later, Jeff and I were in my van in the hospital parking lot. I put the car in reverse to begin backing out.

"Mom, don't back up. There's someone behind you," Jeff said. I stopped, surprised that Jeff had seen a pedestrian that I hadn't noticed. He had been rocking back and forth in a stupor.

I was also amazed to see a piece of paper with a phone number on it sitting on the dashboard. I hadn't seen it before. I called the number before we left the hospital parking lot.

A man answered the phone and said, "Hello."

"Is this a sober house?" I asked.

"Yes," the man replied.

"I need a place for my son to go," I said. The man told me to bring Jeff right over. We arrived, and the man I'd spoken to on the phone saw how stressed I was and how drunk Jeff was.

"We can't evaluate him until tomorrow," the man told me. "Yet, if you pay the initial entry fee, I'll take him in right now and work out the details later."

With relief, I paid him. The man told me to leave quickly.

As I left, I noticed the men in the sober house. They had barely finished a day of community service and had faces of angels, glowing with contentment and peace. One of them was quite young—almost a boy. When he smiled at me, I knew he'd be kind to Jeff. The sober house was called Casa de Vida, meaning "House of Life."

I drove to the beach, caught my breath, and went home thinking, *If I had to spend these days with Jeff again, I would. I've felt peace, love, and protection throughout these crazy days.*

I had yet to learn the outcome of Jeff's stay in Casa de Vida. Yet Jeff would talk about the place, with respect, for years after.

CHAPTER TEN

I would have sung for joy when I drove away from Casa de Vida, but I could not open my mouth to sing. Something was holding me back. When I pulled into my driveway in Simi Valley, I could barely move. I went to bed and picked up El Libro. I read of God's voice speaking from a pillar of fire. I had seen no fire. I had heard no booming voice. Yet, I couldn't have experienced God more powerfully than I did those twelve days at the harbor with Jeff.

It was a miracle that Jeff walked into Casa de Vida—a rehab that I never heard of until its number appeared in my car.

The next morning, my son Phil gave me a CD entitled, "Lullabies for Adults." I listened to it as I lay on my bed and cried. Thoughts ricocheted in my brain. Although I had peace, my mind was ill. The 12 days at the harbor were too much for me to process. If it weren't for the sweet music Phil gave me, I would have felt overwhelmed.

The warmth of sunlight flooded through my window as I read in El Libro: *God carries our sorrow. He was wounded for us. Fear not. I will heal thee.*

Later, my family drove in two cars to Yerba Buena Canyon in the Santa Monica Mountains. We were headed for my favorite hiking trail—The Grotto—at Circle X Ranch. The Grotto is in an alcove of a river with underground water caves. Our youngest family member, Matthew, almost didn't come. Yet, I insisted that we wait for him to get back from the gym to join us. I wanted to keep what's left of my family together.

Matt, Phil and James rode with Greg in the Honda. I rode in Tim's Mazda beside his baby to avoid conversation. I was too tired to talk after my ordeal with Jeff. Yet I smiled when Greg blew a kiss to me from his car.

At the Circle X Ranch we began our hike along canyon streams, cliffs, and waterfalls. The trees appeared to have little lights on them; each glowing leaf caught the sun's reflection.

It is hazardous to reach the caves at the Grotto. You have to lower yourself down a 10 foot drop by hanging onto rocks and tree roots. It scares me, yet I always climb down so I can get into the caves. Once there, I stay as long as I can.

Phil stood in a pool of water singing, "Rub-a-dub-dub," at the entrance to one cave as a waterfall splashed over his head.

My family explored further downstream while I rested in a water cave. I laid down on smooth pebbles beside the pool of clear water. Light shone in from a waterfall at the back of the cave, illuminating pebbles of every color in the water. I listened to the gurgling of water, and the sound of my own breathing. An orange newt looked at me while I looked at it. It reminded me of the Salamander-type creatures that Jeff used to keep in his aquariums. My heart began to heal.

Back at home, I dropped an envelope in the mailbox. It was filled with letters and hand-drawn pictures addressed to Jeff at Casa de Vida. Greg, Phil, Matt, James, and Tim's family contributed. Even Baby Orion shared his handprint in his first letter to Jeff.

The next day, I decided not to let Diane wire Jeff money again. Repeatedly, the cash from his disability checks sent him to the hospital with an overdose. I went to the Social Security Office. I wanted to change Jeff's payee from Diane to Casa de Vida. Casa de Vida does not allow their residents to have money in their own possession. If a resident goes shopping, or anywhere away from the safety of the group, he or she has to have an escort.

There was a crowd of people at the Social Security Office. I entered, and signed in. I was glad when a man's voice called me to the counter. I had hoped that the man would be sympathetic with a woman in distress. Yet, when I met him, his looks didn't match his voice. He had a detached way about him, as if he hated seeing customers.

"It's your son's choice whether or not to use his disability money for drugs," he told me when I explained the situation. "You can't control his life. He'll change when he wants to." Then, to my dismay, he added, "There's no way to make Jeff's money go directly to Casa de Vida unless someone comes here personally from the home. You are his mother, so you can have his disability money placed in your name and then change it to the rehab later."

It wasn't as I had planned, but with Jeff living at Casa de Vida, my life would not be in danger for intercepting his 'drug money.' I let the man transfer Jeff's disability from Diane's name to mine.

I rose to my feet after he finished. A thought entered my mind and I asked, "Could you just stop paying Jeff's disability money—" The man cut me off, saying, "Next," as he stared past me toward the next person in line.

The next day, Bridgett called. "I'm worried about Jeff. He doesn't look good," she said.

"What?" I replied, "He's supposed to be in a rehab!" I called Casa de Vida to find out what went wrong. I learned that Jeff had walked out three hours after I left him there.

Fear shot through me. I was glad that I told no one that I'm Jeff's payee. In order to keep my family safe, I didn't even tell Greg.

If Jeff asks about his money, I'll say it's been rerouted to go to Casa de Vida—without telling him that I'm the middle man.

A few days later, Matt handed me his straight A report card and his plans for his Eagle Scout project. He would organize a drive to collect thousands of canned goods for the needy. Not long ago, Matt had been getting all D's and F's in school and was drinking with the neighborhood boys. So I told Matt he couldn't get his driver's license unless he got all A's and B's. After not speaking to me for 3 weeks, he decided to change.

When Matt got an A on his Math test—and the highest score in the class—a pretty girl, Emily, was upset. It was the first time someone got a higher score than her. Then she saw who topped her, and she was impressed.

Emily—a country girl in blue jeans, boots, a plaid shirt, and long golden brown pigtails—was an answer to my prayers. I'd spent many days praying that a nice girl would distract Matt from his drinking buddies.

'Happy over Matt's straight A report card, I felt energized enough to walk into the kitchen. Once there, I noticed things needed cleaning up, and without warning, I got mad and threw a cup across the room. Ashamed, I walked out of the kitchen, and went to bed. Stress was messing with my brain. All I could think of was that Jeff's disability funds were in my name. I remembered my loved ones telling me, "Don't get involved. Being Jeff's payee would be suicide." The next week we had a comedy theatre in our home. Matt made a video for school—a murder mystery starring Phil. I watched the actors arrive excitedly. Then, they grossed me out with a slit throat, a drowning, a bow and arrow, and electric beaters used by the murderer Phil—who always makes me laugh.

The next morning, Greg slept with his hand in mine as I lay awake listening to the rain pounding on our roof. We got 3 inches of rain in just a few hours. I thought of Jeff camping in the hills and felt helpless.

Then we got a call from Hillmont Psychiatric Hospital. The police had found Jeff lying in a flooded street, incoherent. They couldn't get much out of him. They asked me to visit him.

I went to the Hospital. Jeff didn't wake up during visiting hours. So I went to the sea. There had been an earthquake in Chile that night. The tide was 6 feet lower than normal. I sat there beside the water and called more rehabs in search of an opening for Jeff—to no avail.

Greg saw my sorrow over Jeff's condition. He said, in an attempt to help, "Jeff should just stay in the psychiatric hospital indefinitely."

Instantly, I felt angry. In my former years of suffering from mental illness, I'd been in a mental hospital and it didn't help.

I felt so alone. I didn't talk much when Greg took me to a temple in Los Angeles. On the way home, he sang lullabies to me and I fell asleep with my head on his lap. Then Butterfly called and woke me up. "Have you ever thought you might be enabling Jeff?" she asked. "He needs to want to recover."

I wondered. *Does he want to? I know he tries when he's with me. If he wants help, I'll help him.*

Jeff's 72-hour hospitalization ended. It had taken me five days to unpack from my stay at the harbor. Now I was packing up again, preparing to leave. My friend Karen offered to drop both Jeff and me off at the harbor—if I felt safe. If the situation frightened me, then our plan was that she would drop off only Jeff, and I would return home without him. I ended up staying at the harbor.

While staying overnight on the boat with Jeff, I dreamt that I held a colorful bird in my arms. The size of a chicken, it was cuddly and soft. Its color was bright orange, bordered by black in a marvelous pattern like a maze. It was nice to not have a nightmare. I seem to sleep better when Jeff's not drinking.

Jeff called Freedom House and then invited some missionaries to join us for dinner. "We can take them to a nice Italian restaurant I noticed next to the liquor store called, "The Italian Job Café."

Jeff continued to not drink. His depression from withdrawal from alcohol reminded me of when he lived in Orderville, Utah 2005. There, he didn't get out of bed for weeks. Then he adjusted to alcohol-free living by volunteering for community service. Such an adjustment takes time.

Greg and I took our evening walk together 40 miles apart while talking on the phone. It was heavenly, with parrots in the palm trees, crashing waves, bird songs, and a sense of serenity that only nature can bring. During the day, while scrubbing our boat, I pretended angels were quietly helping.

Later, it began raining while Jeff was working on our boat. He was trying to fix the starboard and port lights. If he got the lights to work, they would enable us to cross the harbor in the dark to get to the evening AA meeting at Peninsula Park. Since we had been dropped off at the harbor by my friend Karen, we had no car to drive. Jeff tested the wires for the boat lights. They were good. Yet, something in the light box wasn't working.

About that time, I plugged an extension cord into the power outlet of the dock and all the electricity in Channel Islands Harbor went out.

"Unplug the cord and see if the power comes back on," Jeff said. "You may have caused the outage when you plugged the cord in."

The rainstorm continued and our battery-operated cabin light was the only light on the dock. Jeff teased me about causing the harbor's power failure. I wondered, *Did I?*

Jeff and I have slept in the boat for two nights. Then, Jeff wrote a letter to his probation officer.

Diary Entry: *Court is tomorrow. Today Jeff did plumbing and electric repairs and caulked a leak above the cabin. He's a good worker when not drinking. Then, he took a walk. When he returned, he stashed a bag somewhere outside and then helped me fill up the water tank for the last time.*

The next day it rained. Too tired to get out of bed, I felt peace just resting. Jeff and I had a prayer. Then I thanked Jeff for not drinking as much. He replied, "You're welcome. I'm trying." Then he took a walk.

That night, Jeff came back onto the boat drunk. A call to Freedom House confirmed that they may have an opening in the morning. Yet Jeff showed no interest. Rather, he excitedly said, "Mom, once I saw a dandelion on the top of a stem that was 4 feet tall." Then he pulled out of his pocket a vodka bottle and took a swig. I handed him his coat and boots and said, "Come back when you're sober."

Voices of sailors returning from sea blended with the howl of the wind as I watched Jeff walk away and get smaller and smaller in the distance.

I remembered my friend Karen saying, "You will need a reality check one day. Helping Jeff may be unreasonable. Maybe he does the right thing only because he's with you. On his own he may not want what's right. You need to let him stand on his own two feet and choose his way when you are not there." A few hours later, Jeff hadn't returned. Roger, who keeps a boat next to mine, said, "Be gentle on him." And I recalled a boy sitting on a bench outside the psychiatric hospital while Jeff was a patient there. The boy told me, "Just love him!"

Yet, I'm scared when Jeff drinks. I'm not myself. Earlier today, Jeff and I had been walking when he asked for my phone. I was afraid he'd throw it in the water. So I said, "I left it on the boat," and hoped it wouldn't ring. It was in my pocket.

I usually don't lie. The next morning I attended a sunrise AA meeting where a woman in the meeting said she lost her children because of her drinking. "I am three days sober," she announced, with tears in her eyes.

I donated some coins to the cup after the meeting, took a donut, and walked away, wanting to lie on the sand and sleep. Yet, I was too tired to walk to the shore. So I reclined on a bench outside a realtor's office, on an abandoned patio. I wanted to be alone.

A bird sang a lovely song overhead. Then lots of birds began singing— more than I've ever heard before. It's spring. The warmth and beauty lifted my heart. Then a thought, as if from God, entered my mind, saying, *Jeff will return.*

I had yet to learn how, when, and where Jeff would return. Yet I felt peace.

I walked to the shore, watched for dolphins, and slept on the sand. Jeff's twin brother Tim found me there and took me to another shore where he began surfing.

Watching Tim and the other surfers ride the waves cheered my heart more than words can say.

That night, back on our boat alone, I was scared. I thought of Jeff's ex-girlfriend stabbing her mother to death. I was afraid to fall asleep, not knowing what mood Jeff might be in if he came back. I took my blanket and spent the night safely locked in the shower stall of the restroom on the shore.

The next day Jeff had not returned. We were due to meet the missionaries that afternoon for dinner at "The Italian Job Café". I went alone. It gave me the incentive to smile and to comb my hair—for the life had nearly gone out of me.

> *Trying to help Jeff, in a sense, gives me a reason to live.*
> *One day I'll be able to say: I've done all I can. I'll find closure.*

After a peaceful dinner with the missionaries at the restaurant, Greg called.

"I checked the jail log," Greg said. "Jeff is in jail."

CHAPTER ELEVEN

The times that Jeff was arrested for public intoxication reached nearly one hundred. I was happy that on Christmas Day, Jeff was out of jail. We agreed to meet beside an auto parts store so that I could give him his Christmas presents.

I waited until I saw him, walking slowly, and downtrodden. It was cold outside and he didn't have any shoes on his muddy feet. I offered to pour water on his feet to clean them, but he refused. I handed him a blanket, flashlight, water, food, and clothes. He took them and walked on.

The next day, Jeff's three-year restraining order ended. Butterfly, Dragonfly, and their four little girls flew in from Kentucky.

The day after Butterfly's family arrived, Jeff knocked on our door.

"Don't come in," Greg told Jeff, taking the side of caution. "Let's talk in the driveway." Butterfly heard Greg and Jeff talking and her face lit up. She ran out the door literally jumping up and down, saying, "It's so good to see you!"

Jeff's hair was matted, his clothing torn and stinky, but no one cared. One by one Tim, Dragonfly, Matt, James and Phil joined us in the driveway. Jeff slurred when he talked and complained about not coming in the house because the restraining order had ended. But we were together, in a strange sort of way, and happiness filled our hearts.

Butterfly and Dragonfly took Jeff for a drive and he showed them where he lived. Butterfly saw one of her friends from school in the homeless camps, eight months pregnant and living in a tent.

"Those people are drug addicts," Butterfly told me when she came home.

"What about Jeff's friend Leta?" I asked. "Jeff tells me that Leta likes to read, and she delivers babies for homeless girls. She also dislikes it when Jeff drinks and she never drinks herself. I spoke to her on the phone once. She sounded nice."

Butterfly replied, "She's probably a drug addict too."

A week later we planned a family dinner at Marie Calendar's Restaurant. Greg and I were ill and couldn't go. Butterfly didn't invite Jeff. "After seeing him inebriated on Christmas Day, I didn't want him around my children," she said.

They were ready to leave for dinner when Jeff called. I answered the phone. His voice sounded different. I handed the phone to Butterfly.

"I'm not on drugs. Someone stole my drugs on New Year's Eve," Jeff told his sister. "I'd like to see you."

"Hey, do you want to come to Marie Calendar's?" Butterfly asked him. "You don't have anything clean to wear? I'll bring you a shirt."

All seven of our children were together that night. Jeff poured vodka into his milk but no one complained and he didn't break any glass. Before leaving the restaurant, Butterfly took Jeff's hands in hers, looked him in the eye and told him, "I have something to ask of you."

"What's that?" Jeff asked, willing to do anything for his sister.

"Stay alive," Butterfly replied.

Jeff looked at her like she had asked him to do a very difficult thing.

The next day, as Butterfly's children were getting ready to catch their flight back to Kentucky, I asked my seven-year-old granddaughter Abby, "Did you like seeing Jeff?"

"Yes," she replied with her southern drawl and an innocent look in her eyes. "It was nice."

"Was he wearing clean clothes?" I asked.

"No, he was dirty," she answered casually, as if I was asking her about the weather. Then she looked at me, as if trying to decide whether it was safe to be honest. Then she said, "Well, I had to hold my nose while he rode with us in the car."

In January of 2011, I invited Jeff to see a St. George, Utah Condo which Greg had rented as a home away from home next door to my mother. "I don't want to go to Utah," Jeff replied.

I conceded to take the trip without him and slipped into bed for a good night's sleep before leaving.

Suddenly, the phone rang. "Have you left for Utah yet?" Jeff asked.

"No, not til morning."

"Can I go with you?"

"Yes. I'll pick you up tomorrow," I replied. Then I drifted back to sleep, comfortable and warm, as the temperature outside dropped toward freezing.

The phone rang again, "Can you pick me up now? I'm behind Jack in the Box." I drove there to pick him up. When he saw me, he said, "I'm glad you came. I slept on the sidewalk here last night and it was really cold."

I recalled that five years earlier on our way to Utah he had frostbitten hands. Once more I could share the warmth of my van with him.

I drove Jeff home from Jack in the Box and gave him an electric blanket. With his blanket cord plugged into our garage outlet, I let him sleep in my van for the rest of the night.

At sunrise, we were on our way. Jeff woke as we passed a liquor store and said, "I won't drink while I'm in Utah."

Jeff felt right at home with the mountain air and the comfort of our condo—and with visiting his grandma and the thrift stores. His temper flared only once over the attorney setting up restrictions on his use of disability money. We were driving to his favorite thrift store at the time, and he hit a window. Softly. No damage done. Then, his acceptance of the fact sunk in.

Time stood still in a healing way at our serene, quiet condo. Jeff stayed in bed while coping with the depression resulting from withdrawal.

Then, Jeff got out of bed to take our neighbor Hal to an all-you-can-eat restaurant. Although Hal worked his upper body at the gym, his legs were crippled with spina bifida. Over dinner, he invited Jeff to go to the gym with him. Yet Jeff didn't answer. He was having trouble concentrating. He took a few bites of food, said he felt sick, and went to the car to lie down until Hal and I finished eating.

The next day, Jeff and I bought farm produce from a stand where I noticed a woman staring at us. As we left the stand to get in our car, she came up to us.

"I know this sounds crazy, but I have to tell you that there is something special about your son." she said. Then she spoke to Jeff with tears in her eyes, "I couldn't stop myself from staring at you—and it's not your height, but your heart. When I saw you, a feeling came over me telling me that you have an incredibly good heart."

With tears streaming down her cheeks, she said, "You're a special person. I just have to tell you there is hope."

The woman, Mardi, quickly became our friend. "Once my life was a mess and I could have ended up in jail or worse," she said. "But my parents' prayers saved me. Now I have beautiful children and a good husband— after thinking I'd never have a normal life."

She invited us to visit her home where she home-schooled her five children. Her husband manufactured mining equipment for mines all over the world. She offered his assistance in looking out for work for Jeff.

"We have a hobby of collecting books," she said, as I noticed the tattoos on her wrists and arms. "So if you like to read, you can make a fire in the fire place, pick out a book and make yourself at home." Jeff's depression turned to hope. His smile brightened and he held up his head.

We drove back to our condo, drinking in the mountain air and feeling buoyant as we watched the sunset. "Can we stop at a thrift store?" Jeff asked, hitting my soft spot.

Once inside the Catholic Church's thrift store, he found a cart to pull behind his bike—the kind that a mother would pull a child in. "I can carry my stuff in it!" he exclaimed.

Over the years I frequently delivered boxes of food to Jeff. He liked storing up on the basics. He was thinking of using the cart to carry supplies.

We loaded his cart in the van and went back to our condo again.

A few days later Jeff and I drove back to California. Jeff played upbeat music on the radio while he took pictures of the crimson sunset that filled the sky.

Back in Simi, Jeff asked to be dropped off with his bike behind Jack in the Box. We parted with plans to meet in the morning.

The next morning Greg and I drove to Jack in the Box to drop off Jeff's cart. Jeff saw us pull up, walked toward us, and gave me a hug. He was high.

"I, I le-left my bike be-behind some trees," he said. "Ca-can you dri-drive me there?" We let him in our van and Greg drove, following Jeff's directions—which led us around in circles. Jeff admitted he was lost. He kept trying to remember where he left his bike. Finally, he had Greg pull over by some trees. Then Jeff got out of the van and walked into a dense thicket to look for his bike.

Greg and I looked inside his backpack. We saw a big container with a strange liquid and a pipe in it—Meth paraphernalia. My heart sank.

What more could I do? He's an addict and I have no power to stop it.

Yet, in desperation, my imagination ran away with me. I'd seen an ad asking for actors. They needed someone to play the part of Jesus. *Jeff looks the part,* I reasoned. *People in the homeless camps call him Jesus because of his looks. If he got the job, it would help him stay sober. Plus Jeff's always wanted to be in a movie.*

A few days later, I called Bridget and asked for Jeff. She said, "Yes, Jeff's here under the bridge," and she handed the phone to him.

"Would you like to go to a movie audition?" I asked Jeff. "It's a Bible movie and they need someone to play the part of Jesus."

Jeff didn't answer.

Maybe he's thinking about it and considering sobriety, I hoped—even though my idea was unreasonable.

"I'll call you tomorrow," Jeff said with a far off voice.

I hoped that Jeff's life would finally change.

The next day was the anniversary of the day Greg and I met. I awoke and rested my head on his chest and listened to his heart beat. I thought of our years together. Then my thoughts focused on Jeff. *I need to get Jeff to the movie audition,* I told myself.

"Happy Anniversary," Greg said, kissing me and making me forget my daydream. Then I told Greg, "Last night I invited Jeff to go to a movie audition for the part of Jesus. He said he'll call me back today."

Then I looked intently at Greg and said, "I supported you when you got the restraining order. Now I ask for your support in what I do today. If Jeff decides to audition, he'll need a place to stay clean and sober. I ask your permission to let me bring Jeff home, if I feel it's the right thing to do. Trust me."

Greg nodded.

I waited for Jeff to call, dreaming about the audition and thinking of how life takes unexpected turns. Just days before, I'd resigned to Jeff being an addict. Yet after seeing the advertisement for the movie audition I began hoping for a miracle.

Jeff called Monday evening.

"Ahh, I don't want to come to the house," Jeff slurred. "Can you meet me at the Arco Gas Station?"

I ignored the slur in his voice and drove to the gas station, saying to myself, *Miracles happen.*

I arrived and saw Jeff on the curb beside his bike, holding a pink stuffed poodle. Beside him were three trash bags of recycling cans and a Styrofoam food container.

I walked over to him. "I brought you some lasagna," I said, cheerfully offering him a plate.

"Do you have four cents?" Jeff asked, not interested in the food. "I'm four cents short for a beer and the man in the store won't let me buy one unless I have four more cents."

"I didn't bring any money," I replied, looking at the bike that lay at his feet. Inside the spokes was a stuffed Garfield kitty and a beer can.

Jeff motioned to the three large bags at his feet. "These recycling cans are worth a lot of money," he said. Then, with a look of disappointment, he added, "The recycling center just closed. I'm too late to turn the cans in and I need to buy a beer."

He motioned to the Styrofoam box at his side. "I bought Chinese food for Bridget and expected to have enough change left over, but I'm four cents short. I was hoping you had some money. That's why I wanted you to come."

"No. Sorry," I replied.

Not giving up, Jeff walked over to my van and opened the door. I followed and watched as he looked in the cup holders for change, finding none. Next he ran his hand behind the seat cushions and under the seats and found no change.

He silently walked back into the convenience store and spoke to the cashier. He returned looking disappointed.

"You don't have any money?" he asked again.

"No, sorry," I repeated. Jeff opened the glove box. Inside, I saw the letter of recommendation that his boss at St. George Steel wrote, commending his good work and character. As Jeff ran his hand across the bottom of the glove box looking for change, my memory skipped back to when we lived in St. George.

"Why don't you come to Utah with me? Maybe you can get your old job back at the Steel Mill," I urged. I reached into the glove box, pulled out the letter, and held it up proudly. "I'd be happy to see you get your job back!"

Jeff pushed the letter aside. "I don't care about getting my job back!" he shouted, thrusting his fist forward and hitting the windshield.

A chill shot up my spine as cracks spread across the glass.

Jeff looked at the window in shock. He opened his fist and looked down at his hand. Then he lifted his hand gently and touched the crumpled glass, saying, "It's okay Mom. Everything's okay. Don't worry."

Then he walked to a trash can between the gas pumps and with garbage flying everywhere, desperately looked for four cents.

He just smashed my windshield and all he cares about is getting a beer, I shuddered, watching him continue his desperate search. He turned to the other trash cans, ignoring the people lined up to buy gas.

His addiction is going to kill him if he doesn't get help, I told myself as I sank to the curb and struggled to steady my finger long enough to press 911.

I told dispatch, "My son just broke my windshield."

I almost dropped my phone when I thought, *Will Jeff get mad at me for calling the police?*

I added, "I'm scared. Hurry!"

I hung up and ran inside the store seeking security beside the cashier—a large man wearing a white turban on his head.

"I just called the police on my son," I told him.

He looked out the window at the flying trash.

"Good thing," he said.

Jeff looked in our direction and I held my breath as he came near. Yet he stopped at the trash container outside the door. As he searched the trash, I slipped past him, got in my van, bowed my head, and prayed. I hoped I was doing the right thing by calling the police. I just wanted him to get help. Tears flowed freely down my face.

Suddenly I heard a scuffle. I couldn't see where it came from.

"I'm not breaking the law!" I heard Jeff shout.

I heard a crack and a thud and stepped out of my van in alarm to see Jeff doubled over on the ground rolling back and forth. I wanted to scream and run to him, but I stood frozen in shock.

"You hit me," Jeff cried, writhing beneath the policeman who stood above him with a club. I buried my head in my hands and tried to understand what was happening.

Oh God, don't let my son be hurt, I cried.

A minute later a stout, short policeman walked up to me, perspiration beading his face.

"I handcuffed your son," he said. "He's in the backseat of the police car. When I approached him he was bent over and when he stood up his height scared me. I thought he was going to lunge at me so I hit his legs with my baton to knock him over," he apologized. "I'll take him to the hospital on the way to the jail to check for injuries. There are several warrants for his arrest—warrants for not appearing in court when he was summoned."

The policeman looked at my windshield and said, "I was there when he kicked out that windshield on Halloween night."

"All I want is for him to be in a place where he can detox," I said between sobs.

The policeman looked at me sympathetically, took pictures of my windshield, and then took Jeff to jail.

I drove home with a heavy heart. I was so sad that I couldn't talk about what happened. I fell asleep beside Greg but woke up at midnight in a cold sweat. Greg gently put his arm around me and stroked my hair. I told him about Jeff's arrest.

"I'm afraid Jeff could have gotten his teeth knocked out when he hit the ground, or broke his nose. I heard his cry when he fell," I told Greg.

Greg replied, "You need to decide whether or not you will have contact with him. How many windows has he broken?"

"What?" I replied in alarm. "Jeff has broken windows and they can be fixed. It's not the windows I'm concerned about. I'm concerned about Jeff's life!"

Greg reached out for me but I turned my back to him and stared off into the night. There were no words to explain how I felt. Greg placed his hand on my shoulder for a few minutes and then rolled over and went back to sleep. I fell asleep too. Then I was jolted awake by Jeff hitting the ground in my dreams. In my dream I was sure he'd been shot.

The next day, Jeff was scheduled for a trial. Yet, after taking one look at Jeff's disheveled hair, and blank stare, the judge postponed the sentencing until the next week.

During our jail visit, I mentioned the movie audition to Jeff. He got mad. He turned his back on me and pressed against the door until a guard came and lead him away.

I felt crushed when Jeff turned his back on me. I wanted to turn my back on him. Yet I awoke the next morning and prayed, and my bitterness dissolved. A thought entered my mind, *Check to see if Jeff's visiting hours are today.* I checked and saw that he was open for a visit. In a flash I jumped out of bed, my heart filling up with love, and my body with energy.

Will he turn his back on me again? I wondered as I walked into the visiting room.

"I didn't think you'd come back," he said. "I'm sorry I got mad." It was obvious that he was happy to see me!

Then he said, "The beer I needed four cents for was not for me. It was for Bridget. She gave me money to buy her some Chinese food and asked me to buy her a beer with the change. I was just trying to keep my promise."

I felt bad for thinking he had an insane thirst for beer on the night of his arrest. He was trying to keep his promise, like always, to the women in the hills. Whether as water boy, food deliverer—or in this case beer deliverer—he'd nearly die trying to help someone.

Later, Jeff entered the courtroom well groomed. No one noticed but me. The judge hardly looked up before putting off the sentencing for one more week.

"I'll be happy to take you to Second Nature," I told Jeff the next time we visited. "It's a Wilderness Rehab near St. George. My brothers went to one once. They butchered a hog, ate squirrel, had no electricity, and came home appreciative and hard working. They say it can cure drug addiction."

"I'll think about it," he replied.

When our visit ended, I called the Wilderness Rehab, Second Nature, to inquire about admitting Jeff. Then I called the movie producers and apologized for Jeff having missed the audition. The producer said, "Send us a video, we still haven't found someone to play the part of Jesus."

Later, I visited with some people at church who knew Jeff. A crippled woman said she appreciated the times Jeff took her to the doctor. He made sure she didn't fall as she used her walker with unsteady steps. She told me she prays for him.

The next month, the judge postponed giving Jeff a sentence again. She wanted to gather more information about Jeff's mental health.

I went jogging before coming to court. Phil often gave me a ride to jail between his classes at Channel Islands College. But this time, in preparation for my next marathon, I ran ten miles from the college to the jail, passing a fat toad, a river, and a huge California condor. After my jog, I waited for court to begin and overheard a conversation between Jeff and his public defender.

"My Mom was giving me a hard time. It's her fault that I broke the window," he said. Then he glanced my way and noticed me sitting there. He got a sad look on his face and I wondered if he was sorry that he tried to shift the blame on me.

Jeff's sentencing was postponed again. I left the courtroom and drove to see our former sailboat Dream Reviver. We had donated her to Freedom House because Jeff wasn't using the boat, and the rest of our family was too busy to sail. She looked clean and in good repair. Missing my sailing days with Jeff, I took comfort in thinking that the clients at Freedom House enjoyed sailing and fishing on our boat.

The next week, I visited Jeff in jail and mentioned the movie audition. I was thinking of applying for a part too. He got upset and threw his chair across the visiting room, ending our visit.

Later, I received a letter from Jeff:

Sorrey I wasint in a good mude the other day.
I wanted to tallk about a copoll things butt I thot you wore in UT and didn't xpeckt you two cum so soon. Owell tell every Budey I say Hi.
Love, Jeff

Later, Jeff called to ask about his twin brother. "How's Tim's family? Has his wife had her baby yet?" Then he named the rest of his brothers and sisters, leaving none out, and asked how they were doing.

I was surprised to get another call from Jeff in which—with a voice touching my heart—he read the audition script which I had mailed to him. I marveled that his voice sounded sweet, gentle, penetrating, and piercing.

Chapter Twelve

Years ago, I attended a seminar on autism. One speaker said, "The autistic child is hypersensitive like a canary in a mine shaft who warns miners of poisonous gases by being the first to get sick."

Jeff is like the canary, except he escapes the poison by flying away into the innocent world of nature. Jeff went to Second Nature Wilderness Rehab for his latest retreat—in Dixie National Forest. It came to an end all too soon.

On May 9, I drove my van across muddy dirt roads where Arizona, Nevada, and Utah meet. In the wilderness I shared Jeff's last day with him; Greg and I had visited him together the month before. The sky was as blue as a Caribbean Sea, the mountain air tasted fresh and clean, and a breeze blew a low whistle. In serenity, we explored the forest. Then we camped under the stars in the wilderness. Beside Jeff's camp was a wild mustang skull sitting on the ground. "I've been carrying it for fifty miles, waiting for you to come and take it home," he told me. *I pictured the perfectly formed skull of a wild mustang as an ornament in our garden.*

The next morning, Jeff's Counselor Mike told me, "You're the only parent to come into this wilderness more than once."

That's odd, I thought. *Why wouldn't every parent want to come into such a beautiful and quiet place, away from the stress of life?*

Having had a good night's sleep, I was ready for more exploration. I took off alone and got lost. I walked in circles until a counselor named Red Hawk found me and showed me the way back to camp. The frightening experience of getting lost was nothing compared to my next adventure with Jeff. The hardest journey was about to begin. Soon, Jeff would be living with me in our St. George, Utah condo and attending Dixie Technical College—something he planned during his wilderness rehab. In the wilderness he had been tested by a psychologist and found to be gifted mechanically, and also autistic. His diagnosis answered years of unanswered questions.

"Can I drive?" Jeff asked as we left Second Nature. Then he added, knowing his license was lost when he got his last DUI, "It's only a dirt road. You can drive when we get to public land." I gave in and let him drive—like I did when he was 16. Back then I hesitated at first because of his learning disabilities, but I felt a whisper in my heart say, *It's important for Jeff to have a car.*

I savored our freedom as Jeff drove through the forest. I endured his fast driving, asking him only a few times to slow down. Then we made it to the paved road, and I took the wheel.

On May 14, 2011 I wrote: Today is Jeff's fourth day of living in our Utah Condo. I'm nervous and hopeful. I helped Jeff sign up for Diesel Engine courses at Dixie Technical College. He brought home fifty pounds of books. Each day is like a marathon as we run errands to prepare for college.

Jeff and I took a drive to Zion National Park's Flute Festival. One of its attractions was my brother-in-law Martin Tyner's golden eagle which he resuscitated after it nearly drowned. I'd seen a picture of what the eagle looked like when Martin pulled it out of a flood canal. Its head hung limp as if it were dead. It reminded me of Jeff before he quit using drugs. Now both Jeff and the eagle were strong and healthy.

"I'm happy to see you," Martin told Jeff. "I hope you will have a good time in Utah."

Jeff replied politely, "Thank you." I hoped this was a good beginning.

Jeff's Counselor Mike from the Second Nature Rehab continued visiting Jeff weekly at our condo. He said that with Jeff's 5% social skills, it would be better for Jeff to attend church instead of Recovery Meetings. The recovering addicts would be a bad influence on him. From past experience, I felt it was wrong to make our kids attend church when they didn't want to. I hoped Jeff would choose to go on his own. I went against Mike's advice and required Jeff to attend Recovery Meetings.

At the first meeting someone asked Jeff, "How long have you been sober?"

"Four months," Jeff replied.

"Wow. How did you do it?" the person asked.

"I was in jail," Jeff replied.

The person let out a knowing laugh.

As the meeting progressed, I stared out the window at the sunset. A red glow emanated from the mountains. The swaying palms and dancing aspens mesmerized me. A few drops of rain fell into a pool outside the window. Inside, someone turned out the lights and lit candles. People shared their recovery stories. I looked at Jeff and the other recovering addicts. Their faces were glowing.

Jeff and I went to Twelve-Step meetings in seven different locations— one location for each day of the week. In a nearby town, the elderly husband and wife who led the meeting brought a home-cooked feast from their farm. A man Jeff's age brought his guitar and sang a song he wrote about his new life after recovery. Jeff listened politely, but spoke little. I wished he would make friends.

The first week of school Jeff eagerly rode his bicycle to class. He'd already read his treasured textbooks. A couch warmer like me, Jeff's love of books matched my own. Also being a homebody like me, he helped with laundry, vacuuming, cooking and household repairs.

By June 2011 it was time for Jeff to go to court in California. Greg came to Utah and drove the three of us straight to Ventura's Courthouse. He didn't risk driving through Simi Valley where Jeff's drug-using friends lived.

In court, the judge said, "Jeff should go back to Utah and finish his schooling there—and stay away from California."

Jeff's probation officer gave him a travel permit to return to Utah.

The officer looked at Greg and me, "Whatever it takes to keep Jeff out of California, do it," he said. Then he filed a request to have Jeff's three-year-probation rerouted to Utah. Greg drove us straight to our Utah condo during the night.

The next week I learned that Utah's probation department refused to take Jeff on as one of their clients. "One of his charges is domestic violence," the officer explained. "We don't take domestic violence cases from other states."

I researched laws and procedures and made a plan to help Jeff stay in Utah. I went to California and made my case in court. "Utah will not offer Jeff probation unless you reverse the domestic violence order," I told the judge. "The window broken on January 16, 2011 was not an act of violence aimed toward me. Jeff's unable to communicate his feelings. He's at a loss to let others know what he needs. He loves to help people and on occasion has saved my life—like when he took the wheel when his brother fell asleep while driving. Jeff doesn't want to make trouble. He goes out of his way to avoid getting on other people's nerves. He'd give anything to have us know he doesn't want to hurt anybody." The judge removed the domestic violence charge.

A few months later, Utah probation was ready to take Jeff's case on. Then they found out that Jeff was already living in Utah. "We can't procure Jeff's probation," the Utah probation officer said, "because the law says a prospective client is not supposed to live in our state until after we finish our investigation of his case."

I was frustrated, yet I didn't give up. With the help of California probation, I continued getting travel permits for Jeff so that he could continue going to school.

"Keep him in Utah," the officers from California said. "He doesn't have to live in California while the transfer process is going on."

I looked up the law and as it turned out, Utah was right. Jeff was not supposed to be there. Jeff and I were stuck. Both states wanted him in the other state.

With Jeff's California probation officer being three hundred miles away, I was on my own in supervising Jeff. I tried to support the California court's verdict that Jeff get counseling, have no drugs or alcohol, not enter bars, and not associate with anyone with a drug problem or a felony.

One day I gave Jeff money to buy his lunch at school. I hoped I could trust him. After school he biked to the gym and then all over town. He returned home excitedly announcing, "I found a free canoe and a free stuffed pony at a yard sale. We should get them for my nieces and nephews."

I was too tired to look—until my cell phone rang. It was Phil calling to see how we were doing.

"I'm too tired to drive Jeff places anymore," I told Phil.

"Help Jeff if he needs your help. It shouldn't be that hard. Just make up your mind to do it," Phil encouraged.

I forced myself to get up and drive Jeff to where he wanted to go. We looked at the canoe. It was a monstrous thing that never would have fit in our garage. The pony had been taken by someone else at the yard sale before we got there. "It was big enough for all of my nieces and nephews to climb on at the same time," Jeff said with disappointment when he saw that it was gone. As we were leaving the yard sale, Jeff saw a motorcycle. It was the first of many motorcycles that he would look at.

Back at our condo, Jeff was subdued. I thought it odd until I found an empty water bottle that smelled like vodka. He had used his lunch money to buy liquor.

"You need to go to the 12 step meeting tonight," I told Jeff.

We walked into the meeting and Jeff sat in the back of the room with a hard look on his face.

"I feel like throwing in the towel," I told a friend whose husband was an addict.

"Most people would do that," she said. "But you have a special kind of faith that keeps you going. Don't abandon your son. He needs you."

By the end of the meeting the impenetrable look on Jeff's face had softened. He had come out of his dark and scary place. Hope had returned.

The next Sunday Jeff announced, "I'm going to church today." Thrilled, I envisioned him meeting men and women who would be nice to him.

A moment later my mother, who lived next to our condo, walked in. I thought she'd be happy when I told her that Jeff was going to go to church. She looked at Jeff's blue jeans with a tear at the knee, and exclaimed, "You can't come to church dressed like that!"

"But he hasn't done this week's laundry yet," I told my mom, "These are his cleanest pair of pants. He can be encouraged to dress better when we have more time."

"Then don't sit by me," she said.

Some people say it's the "old school" in my Mom that made her stress out over how Jeff dressed for church. But I felt she was sadly missing a great opportunity to sit by a special person who was taking a huge step in a direction that could change his life for the better.

CHAPTER THIRTEEN

The summer temperature in Saint George approached 110 degrees so Jeff and I escaped the heat by driving to Pine Mountain. The rich smell of pine needles greeted us as we stepped out onto the melting snow, which fed lush ferns, streams, and waterfalls.

Later, while driving home in the heat, I poured water on my head to keep myself from falling asleep at the wheel. Then, two blocks from our condo, I almost pulled in front of a speeding car, but Jeff stopped me, saying "Don't go!"

Back at home, Jeff worked on his bicycle. Then he got a waterfall going in our backyard pond. At 9 PM he went to a dance for singles at a nearby church. He was a handsome sight, going to his first dance in twenty years.

At midnight he came home wearing a black hat that made him look like Abe Lincoln. Someone at the dance had given it to him. He had a big grin on his face as he hung the hat on the head of a stick horse that he kept in our living room.

Nearby, a remote-control airplane hung from our ceiling. He got the plane from a woman named Lynn whom he met at church. Lynn and her husband Don ran a ranch in Circleville, Utah. They invited Jeff to stay at their ranch while I was in California for my next court date on Jeff's behalf. They offered Jeff a part time job on their ranch.

Upon my return to Utah, I was happy to see a delighted Jeff rafting down the Virgin River beside their ranch. I began dreaming of them taking Jeff in permanently so that I could move home with Greg.

On the Fourth of July, Jeff and I drove to Lynn and Don's ranch. Jeff gave me a tour of the guest house which stood beneath a canopy of trees. A sweet scented breeze filled the rooms, along with melodic bird songs.

In the morning—with horses and llamas grazing nearby—Jeff showed me a pond beneath a red cliff on Lynn and Don's property. He gave me food to feed the Koi while he cleaned the pond's filter. Then Jeff spent the rest of the day helping Lynn restore her 1967 lemon yellow VW bug that had a black convertible top. He took us on a successful test drive, and I was proud of him.

Next, Jeff helped Lynn's renter work on his old car. The renter had a few beers, but I didn't see Jeff drink any. *He's learning to be happy without alcohol,* I thought.

That evening was their Fourth of July party. Neighbors came with food for the feast. One family had ten children—all of them home schooled and one autistic. They were vibrant and glowing. I watched an older sister relax beside her autistic brother, seemingly content with silence.

Jeff and Don tied rockets to a tall stack of dried up Christmas trees which their neighbors had given them for this event. At nightfall, with the stroke of a match, the dry Christmas trees whooshed up in flames several stories high. Rockets shot from the trees toward the river. Jeff and the younger autistic boy stood with the men and shot rockets into the air. The fiery popping blaze enthralled me, but not as much as the smile on Jeff's face as he helped light up the dark night.

After the fireworks, Jeff and I drove back toward St. George. I began to fall asleep at the wheel and insisted on staying at a roadside rest. Jeff was anxious to get home. "A Native American girl was murdered at this roadside rest," he told me. I'd heard the stories but stopped there anyway. After sleeping for an hour, I drove home. I noticed a bulge under Jeff's shirt as he anxiously went inside ahead of me and came back out without anything under his shirt. The next morning, Jeff missed school. "I feel sick," he said. I suspected alcohol.

On July 9, 2011 Jeff and I went to California for a court date. After checking his progress, the judge told him to return to Utah. However, Jeff's sister Christy was having a baby shower the next day in Simi Valley and I wanted to share her special event. That night, Jeff suddenly disappeared, along with one of the bicycles from our garage. Then he called me from the hills to tell me he borrowed one of our bikes and wanted to give it back before it got stolen. I left for the hills, hoping to bring him back too.

Jeff met me at the foot of the hills.

"I'm staying in the hills tonight," he announced as he placed the bike in my van. There was nothing I could do to stop him. I watched him walk into the thicket that devoured him, hardly able to bear the thought of losing him.

For the rest of the night I chose to camp in my van at the foot of the hills. At first, I parked on a residential street. In my van bed, I wrote in my diary using my flashlight. Then, as if I was some hoodlum, a man and his wife came and told me to leave their neighborhood. So I went to an industrial center parking lot. I didn't feel safe, until Tim brought me my dog.

In the middle of the night, I heard a car engine. Frightened, I held my breath until the strange car slowly drove away. Then a police car drove up. He circled around and parked beside my van. He got out and shined his flashlight inside the van. I hid under my blanket very still and he left me and my dog alone.

Come morning, I savored the lovely fresh air and realized, *I could almost fit in with the homeless—they sleep close to nature every night.*

My daughter Christy called, worried about me. "I know it sounds crazy for me to be sleeping in my van," I told her, "but if you had a child lost in the woods, wouldn't you want to camp nearby until he was found?"

"Yes," she replied sympathetically.

In a way, the reprieve in my van was my escape from exhaustion. I lied there resting, writing a poem which I gave to Christy at the baby shower.

A mother's love is special
More strong than cords of steel.

Through her love she holds the world
Like a hub holds up a wheel.

A child grows under Mama's care—
Her loving, watchful eye.
Mama gives up her good sleep
To calm her baby's cry.

Your crayons wrote on my walls.
Your shoes tracked in mud pies.
But now you've grown to womanhood
Right before my eyes.

Soon a child will fill those arms
That used to reach for me.
The love we share is deeper now,
For a mother you'll soon be.

During the baby shower, Jeff called. "There's a restaurant that serves free steak to the homeless on the second Sunday of the month. Ask everyone at the house if they want to eat dinner with us there." He sounded sober and I was touched by his desire to share the best of his world with our family. Yet I didn't get back from the baby shower in time to pick him up for the free dinner.

When I arrived at the foot of the hills, Bridget was with him.

"Bridget hasn't eaten yet," Jeff explained.

"Would you like me to bring her home for dinner?" I asked Jeff before she pulled out a container from her pocket and took a swig.

"I don't want to bring Bridget home," Jeff replied, "Let's go to the Samaritan Center for dinner instead."

At the Samaritan Center, Jeff, Bridget and I had a nice meal of chicken, mashed potatoes and salad. As we ate, Jeff talked to some recovered addicts.

"I've been sober for 18 months," one man proudly announced.

Another man said, "I've been sober for 3 months and it's the hardest thing I've ever done. I'm still fighting."

"I hear you're going to a Diesel College in Utah," another man said. Then he added "You should get a Mercedes because a Mercedes has a diesel engine."

"I already got one," Jeff grinned. He had bought a forty-year-old Mercedes for $300 and had it towed to his school. It hadn't been running for 10 years. Yet Jeff got it going the next day. Jeff smiled after mentioning his car. As I watched him eat dinner at the Samaritan Center, I felt relief. The hills had spit him out sober, and we would soon drive back to Utah.

Back in Utah, I drove Jeff to Orderville. He wanted to go to church and see his old friends. Yet he was in a bad mood because I had pulled into a police station on the way, and handed a Sheriff Jeff's home brew that I found in our garage. I could tell Jeff was angry. Before church I visited our friend Granny, and confided, "I'm worried about Jeff. I fear he's going the wrong way."

"If Jeff doesn't go the way you want him to, it's alright," Granny replied. "Be at peace whether he does or not. None of us are perfect."

Jeff and I sat beside Granny's family at church. Her granddaughter, Heidi, had been ill and lost so much weight that I thought Jeff wouldn't recognize her.

When we got in the car to drive home after the service, Jeff said with a big grin, "Heidi's cute." I guess some things just don't fade.

One of our neighbors in the condominium told me, with he his arm around his wife, "What Jeff needs is a good girl. That will keep him out of trouble."

Later, I took Jeff to a ranch for equine therapy—an animal-based therapy for special needs persons. Jeff sat on a bale of hay while waiting for his counselor to arrive. When she came, Jeff smiled, and asked, "How old are you? Are you married?"

The pretty instructor replied, "I'm thirty and single." Then she added, "I'll be moving to Kentucky soon though." That sparked a conversation about Jeff's sister Butterfly. He hadn't even touched the horses yet, and he was already opening up.

Within minutes, Jeff was holding the reins of a huge gray Appaloosa. His instructor discovered that he was gifted with horses. Next, I watched him work in an arena full of horses, trying to capture one. His pretty counselor sat on the corral fence watching. Horses darted in every direction as Jeff calmly moved toward a lovely brown mare. He stroked her head with his big gentle hand. She gave him an affectionate nuzzle. Then Jeff placed a lead rope around her neck and led her to his counselor.

I never dreamed when he was in jail six months ago, that he'd end up working with horses and talking to a pretty girl in a corral. The craziness of his former life dissolved under the Utah sky.

Late that summer, I knelt beside Jeff's closed bedroom door, praying for help. I'd planned to go to the library while Jeff was in school, but was in limbo. He drank the night before and was skipping school again. *Do I wake him, or let him sleep?* I wondered. A thought entered my mind, *Disconnect from his drinking and have faith.* I decided not to worry and went to the library.

On September 21, 2011 I went back to California to be with Greg. Lynn stayed with Jeff at our condo. I was relieved to find Jeff happy and studious when I returned.

Eventually, though, I grew too tired to drive Jeff where he needed to go. I called *Gentle Touch Home Care.* "I need help around the house and with transportation for my son," I told the receptionist, silently praying for them to send a girl that would be good for Jeff.

They sent Sandra to my house—a girl from Colombia. When she arrived to do housework, I thought she was not particularly attractive, but rather plain. Jeff—who had skipped school that day—walked onto our front porch where I was giving her instructions. Jeff and Sandra did a double take when they saw each other.

Jeff went back in the house and Sandra asked, "How old is Jeff? Is he married?"

Later, when she went home, Jeff came out of his room and asked me the same questions, "How old is she? Is she married?"

The next time Sandra came, I noticed her hair. It had been pinned up in a bun before, yet this time it hung down to her waist in a reddish glow.

She also wore make-up and a stunning blue outfit. I hadn't noticed before how beautiful she was.

Is she dressed up to impress Jeff? I wondered.

Unfortunately, when I asked her to drive Jeff to the grocery store for me, Jeff was indignant and walked into his room and slammed the door. Sandra looked confused.

I explained, "Jeff doesn't want you to take him grocery shopping. It hurts his pride to have a hired girl take him to the store."

"Maybe Jeff can drive my car," Sandra replied in her broken English. "I've had my license for a short time in America and I'm scared to death of traffic."

"He's waiting to get his driver's license back after a DUI," I explained. After hearing the word, "DUI," Sandra's hopeful look fell as she began the housecleaning. She attempted to take our big trash can from the garage to the curb. Yet she couldn't open the garage door. I was lying down on the couch and heard the garage door opener start and stop, again and again.

Too tired to get up and check on her, I was relieved when Jeff came out of his room, walked into the garage, and asked Sandra, "Do you need help?"

"I can't get the garage door to open," she replied.

"I'll get it," Jeff said, and he opened the garage door without any trouble. Then he helped Sandra with the trash. After that, he showed her where my mother lived so they could have a little visit. To my mother's delight, they spent an hour together looking at photo albums.

Later, Sandra attempted to bake bread for me, and said, "I can't get the bread loaf pan to fit in the bread mixer."

Jeff was sitting at the kitchen table with a book and said, "Here, I can do it."

"Thank you," Sandra said.

I smiled as Jeff helped her find the butter, honey, yeast and flour. Although I was sick on the couch, I could see sparks fly as Jeff helped my helper.

How convenient for me to not be able to do the housework, I mused.

While the bread was baking, Jeff decided to let Sandra take him shopping after all. While they were gone, the officer from Utah probation that had already denied Jeff twice came back to ask me some questions.

"Jeff has to live outside of the state while we're making our decision," the officer said. I didn't say where Jeff was, and the officer didn't probe. He finished his questioning and left, right before Jeff and Sandra walked through the door.

CHAPTER FOURTEEN

Jeff finally got a Utah probation officer under the condition that I would not go back to California unless I arranged for a guardian for Jeff. Jeff loved it when Sandra agreed to check on him each morning and night while I visited California. "I don't need help with transportation, I can bicycle to school. But I don't mind Sandra calling me or dropping by," he said.

After I returned to Utah, I wrote: I'm lying on a lounge on our patio, watching the stars. The waterfall in Jeff's pond trickles. Crickets chirp. On my cell phone I say to Greg, "Goodnight, I love you." He watches the stars come out too, from three hundred miles away.

A few days later, I heard Jeff cuss in the middle of the night, "No way! You're freakin' crazy," he said to no one. Come morning, Jeff walked into my room as his normal self again. He sat for an hour in a chair next to my bed surfing the internet on my iPhone. He showed me hedge hogs, saying, "I'd like to buy these for Butterfly's family." Then he showed me pictures of ferrets. He'd always wanted to raise some. And, as always, he showed me motorcycles, land for sale, and boats. He read a lengthy description of a sailboat for sale in Mexico.

Then I opened El Libro and read scriptures about hope, after which Jeff prayed, "Help me do good in school."

The head of the department of diesel engine mechanics told me, "Jeff is stinkin' smart! He can figure out engine problems faster than I can and he's helping me teach the other students."

I was happy to give Jeff garage space for working on engines. And even happier when he found a free aquarium filled with over a hundred black mollies. He kept the fish tank clean and shiny in our living room where it reflected light and softly gurgled.

When his mollies gave birth to hundreds of babies, he and Sandra put many in our backyard pond and traded many at Petco for my favorite fish—neon tetras—which Jeff got just for me.

Jeff continued, at times, to succumb to his weakness for alcohol.

At a twelve step meeting, a mother told me that her had son died of a drug overdose. "For a long time I could not find peace," she said. Then, pointing to a painting on the wall, she said, "One day I looked at this painting of pioneers in the snow, laying their child's body in a frozen grave with their other children standing around in ragged clothes. It hit me that many pioneers didn't survive the elements. As the picture took me in, comfort wrapped around me and I knew that it was no more my fault that my son died than it was the pioneer mother's fault that the winter was unusually cold. Some things we just can't help."

Later, I drove Jeff to Zion National Park to pan for gold. I bought his pan at a Prospector's Shop—unable to say no when he asked for it. Jeff found a stream off the beaten road and spent all day panning for gold. The only sound was that of the bubbling waters. A peaceful repose.

Then we drove home and were greeted by hundreds of fish in our aquarium. Jeff rocked in our rocking chair with my iPhone, looking at boats for sale. On the radio in the background bagpipes played *Amazing Grace*. A bird sang outside our open door. The temperature was perfect. I breathed in the delicious air. Heaven embraced us as I said to myself, *This peace is divine. Being with Jeff is a timeless treasure.*

Greg called from California at sunset.

"I'm hiking a trail with woodpeckers in the trees and unusual clouds. Some clouds are wispy. Others look like cotton balls. Others have textures with dots and swirls of purple and green." As Greg spoke, time stood still and our love bridged the gap of three hundred miles.

October 17, 2011, Hurricane, Utah: Moments ago, Jeff walked out of the Department of Motor Vehicles and for the first time in three and a half years, he has a driver's license. I'm riding in the van with Jeff behind the wheel. I lean back to rest, my body relaxed, tension draining out of me. To my amazement, the song *On the Road Again* begins playing on the radio. Jeff's face is set in deep concentration as he drives down the freeway. The music, and the breeze from the open window, add to my delight.

October 20, 2011: Jeff says he wants to go to school, but he just lies in bed. Something is pulling him down. Alcohol, I fear. I kneel outside his bedroom door and pray for him to get up. He isn't getting up. I pray for me to be able to bear the anguish I feel.

A few days later, I invited Sandra to a harvest dinner at our church. When she couldn't find her way there, she parked her car at our condo. We were at the dinner already. She called us for directions. Even though our condo was only one block away, Jeff replied, "Just stay at the condo and I'll come pick you up."

Jeff left, and a few minutes later they returned smiling and joking.

Jeff's friend Blake was at the dinner, and got a big grin when he saw Jeff walk in with a beautiful woman.

"This is my assistant, Sandra, who helps me around the house," I said, introducing her to Blake. Then I added, "I wish Sandra could take my place in caring for Jeff, but probation requires family to stay with him."

"They could get married," Blake said, watching Sandra blush.

"They'd have to fall in love first," I teased.

"Give us a week," Jeff quickly inserted with a grin. Sandra continued blushing until we sat down and enjoyed a wonderful dinner.

The next day Sandra dropped by our condo for Sunday dinner. Her bubbly personality transformed our quiet evening. Sandra told us that when her ex-husband wouldn't turn down the television, she threw the television set down on the floor, breaking it.

"You are a strong woman," I told Sandra. "I like your feisty way of silencing the television."

"My ex-husband called me feisty," Sandra replied, with her strong Colombian accent. "I thought it was a bad word."

We ate tamales that we made with Sandra's recipe, and stayed up late telling stories and laughing. In serious moments, Sandra shared her heart as Jeff and I listened, "I trust God's unseen plans will fill the empty spaces in our lives."

In January 2012, on my next visit to California, Lynn and her ranch dog stayed with Jeff at our condo. Lynn parked her lemon-yellow VW bug that Jeff helped her restore in our garage. Lynn and Jeff were heading for Lynn's hockey league game at the park when I left. Lynn's husband Don was staying at their ranch, so Jeff rooted for Lynn alone.

During the game, an opponent smacked Lynn off her feet and her leg was broken. "You could hear her bone crack," Jeff told me when I returned to Utah and we drove to the hospital to visit her.

"Jeff was great," Lynn told me during our visit. "He was the first to my side after it happened. He helped me get off the rink and then assisted the paramedics when they came. Without his help I wouldn't be doing as well as I am."

Then Lynn asked, "Will you take my dog for a run? She probably feels cooped up at your condo."

Jeff and I returned home and found Lynn's dog lying in our fishpond with her head resting on the rocks above the water. She had an endearing smile that only a dog can give when it gets into mischief. After coaxing her out of the water, Jeff and I drove to Gunlock Reservoir. Water gushed out of the reservoir in seven frothy cascades as Jeff and I explored. Soon the dog brought Jeff a piece of driftwood that looked like a prehistoric bird with outstretched wings. *Another relic for our garden.*

The scenery overpowered me, and I wrote: *The backdrop of the mountains swallows me up, fills my senses, and takes my breath away.*

When it was time to leave, I called the dog. She refused to come. Yet when Jeff called her, she stopped dead in her swim, turned around, and followed us back to the car.

A few days later, Jeff came home smelling like alcohol. Instead of thinking that his relapse came because so and so did such and such, or because something went wrong that wasn't supposed to go wrong, I let it go. *God has saved me from misery in the past. He'll deliver me again.*

I didn't know it at the time, but my third and fourth tumors were starting to affect my brain. They made me exhausted and affected my memory. While I rested in bed, Sandra helped Jeff sign up for Spanish and Welding classes at night school. I hoped Jeff's passion for learning Spanish and welding would offset his interest in alcohol.

Jeff found a good deal on a cell phone and I let him buy it. He also found a broken computer for ten dollars which he got running in no time. Before this, Jeff regularly picked up his mess in his room, the garage, kitchen and living room in order to get permission to use my phone. On the weekends he cleaned the bathroom and vacuumed too. Yet things changed when Jeff got his own phone and computer. He quit doing chores for privileges and the house became a mess. *I don't know how so much went wrong so fast. Maybe it's a combination of things. Jeff met some people who call him for rides. Do they pay for transportation with drugs?* I wondered.

Surprisingly, Jeff continued to be the class genius in college.

"My instructor is considering sending me to Salt Lake City for the Inter-State Diesel Competition. He picks one student each year to go to the event," Jeff told me. I was excited, hoping Jeff's mechanical success would replace the chaos and inebriation that we were beginning to live with.

At school, Jeff's teacher and fellow students continued to check his water bottles for vodka. *Their checking up on Jeff must be helping. Jeff is on schedule to graduate in spring.*

Greg came to visit us in Utah. He could tell that Jeff was on Meth. Both of us were no longer in denial. I tried to put the pieces of our lives together in a picture with a happy ending, but my track record for figuring out the future was bad.

March 15, 2012: Jeff didn't come home for dinner or during the night. Greg and I talked for hours in bed. Greg usually has trouble expressing his emotions, so I cherished him sharing his tender feelings about Jeff.

March 16, 2012: Greg has gone back to California. Jeff is playing with rocks, liquid Drano and brake cleaner. It seems like some sort of Meth concoction. The fumes hurt my nose. I keep waiting for probation to catch him. Jeff's probation officer says that unless they personally catch him using drugs or alcohol, they can't do anything about it.

I asked Jeff to read a page from El Libro. He read—pronouncing and translating the words with increased proficiency. It took the edge off the darkness I felt creeping in.

The next morning, when Jeff awoke, I told him he had to take a drug test which I arranged with a local clinic. Jeff turned his back on me and walked out the door. At that moment, my sister came for a visit. She spoke with Jeff while I parked my van behind his Mercedes so that he couldn't get it out of the driveway until he drug tested. Then my sister and I visited Mom next door.

When we came back outside, we saw that my van had been moved a few feet and Jeff's Mercedes was gone.

I sat on my porch and cried as my sister sat beside me.

"I think Jeff's using Meth," I told her.

"I think so too. I could tell by the way he looked," she said.

Somehow, sharing my concern with my sister made my burden lighter. Her son is a recovered Meth addict, with an even more heartbreaking past than Jeff's because her son had a family that went through it with him.

"When Jeff walks the wrong way," my sister added, "Don't worry. Trust God. Jeff's problems will pass. He's innocent and naïve like a child and will not be held accountable for going the wrong way when his friends lead him astray."

I remembered in Orderville someone told me that Jeff needed a good friend in order to stay sober. I wondered if that good friend is meant to be none other than God.

"There's a purpose for everything," my sister said. "All the childhood abuse and mental illness you've suffered has prepared you to be comfortable with people who have problems. What you went through prepared you to help Jeff. God knew you'd stick by him. That's why He sent Jeff to you."

CHAPTER FIFTEEN

In Spring 2012 Jeff spent a weekend fixing someone's car for free. He didn't know the person's name. I think he was paid in drugs.

Despite his backsliding, we still had some good days. We picked out a motorcycle with a bent frame for his night class' welding project. He welded a new piece onto it to make it as good as new. Then he asked me how to spell words such as "to," "door," and "their" as he typed job applications on his computer.

March 27, 2012: Last night when I asked Jeff to clean up his mess in the kitchen, he threw his chair aside and swung his arm across the counter, hurling the food across the room. Then he went to bed.

Potato chips were scattered across the kitchen floor. His soda can lay on its side in a sticky puddle, and a bottle of mustard was on the floor near where it hit the wall.

That was last night, and I decided to go camping to get away. When I returned from Zion National Park, and walked into our condo, I saw that Jeff hadn't cleaned up his mess of soda, chips and mustard on the floor. His car was gone. I got back in my van and drove to an AA meeting. Someone there said, "Life is meant to have difficulties. They are there for a reason. Sometimes only God knows the purpose. But one day, we will thank Him for our trials."

The next day Jeff announced, "I want to take a break from school." I started to ask, "Why take a break when you're so close to graduation?" but I bit my lip. I was afraid to say anything because he seemed edgy. I sank back in my chair and prayed.

Surprisingly, my first prayer was, *Thank you God for my marriage. When things go wrong, I don't blame anybody, and it feels good.*

Jeff did go to school. The spring day was beautiful. I took a walk and gazed down from a hilltop. Below me I saw an elderly man planting seeds in his garden. Like in *The Tortoise and the Hare* story, the man moved slow but steady. He wiped sweat from his brow while leaning on the hoe. Then he sat on a metal chair to open his next packet of seeds before massaging his neck and planting again.

He looked like he had farmed for eighty years. Surely he'd been a prize for a young lady in his youth. Even in old age he looked good in his Levis jeans, shiny belt buckle, cobalt shirt, and black cowboy hat. Perhaps he'll leave this world in his sleep or in his garden, satisfied over a life well-lived. I hope Jeff and I can grow old like him—working until the end, patiently.

I continued my walk, with increasing love for my son who drinks, uses Meth, and throws food in my kitchen.

When he bought groceries for me, I asked to see his receipts. They didn't add up. When I started to empty the trash, he quickly offered to empty the van's trash. He'd never offered to do that before. I looked where he dumped it and saw an empty vodka bottle, which explained the receipt.

I'm tired of Jeff's addictions. Yet, as the threat of disaster increases, I feel peace. I believe with all my heart that if Jeff or I die, God will heal us and wipe away our tears.

Diary: Jeff just picked me up from a counseling appointment on his way home from school. I sit in silence, clutching my pen, while he drives.

Jeff's driving too fast!
My soul screams, *I'm scared!*
Trust me, I hear God whisper to my heart.
But Jeff's driving like a maniac! I reply.
Be Still, the voice says.

I panic. I'm shaking.
But the voice says,
Be Still.

When we got home, Jeff borrowed my phone. I feared asking him to give it back. I suspected he'd throw it through the window. He's skipping his night class. I'm afraid to ask why. I want to leave. I don't feel safe here. Oh, I am so tired.

Later, Jeff and I were both asleep when his probation officer came in the night. The pounding on our door put me in a panic. After the officer made a surprise search of our condo, and found nothing, he left. But I couldn't go back to sleep. The officer's pounding kept ringing in my ears.

March 31, 2012, Zion National Park. Dawn. I'm filled with joy, my mind at rest. Yesterday, Jeff left in his Mercedes for a camping trip with his friends. One of his friends suggested that I try marijuana to calm myself. Instead, I drove to Zion. As I drove, I recalled a talk I had with Jeff, "These people are not good friends," I reminded him. "They already pawned off one of your bicycles."

Jeff looked concerned.

Later, Jeff called to tell me they had arrived at their campsite safely and everything was fine. I was surprised that he sounded sober. I had imagined him getting caught driving high and losing his license. But none of the bad things I imagined came true.

In Zion, I let the mountains heal me. I smelled the campfire smoke, and listened to the happy voices of children. I remembered the times I'd camped there as a child, and also as a mother.

I thought of my present life in St. George. I was spending most of my days tending Jeff. As a result, my heart was flooded with love. I'd grown to love Greg more deeply as well. Dealing with Jeff united our marriage.

I took a walk to Emerald Pools. I watched millions of drops of water fall from seeping rocks into the pool below. It was dark when I walked away from Emerald Pools to return to my van. A movement in the grass caught my eye. Bending down, I saw a fat toad and took pictures of it. I looked at the photos and was surprised to see that the toad's color changed from green to brown with each picture I took. It reminded me of Jeff—how his behavior adapts to who he's with. After leaving the toad, I crossed a bridge and paused, gazing at the moonlight on the water.

Greg called while I stood there. "Jeff's phone usage went way up last night, around 2 AM," Greg said with frustration. I was too tired to tell Greg about Jeff's camping trip with his friends. I held my phone away from my ear as Greg detailed the time and length of each phone call. Instead of listening closely, I dreamed of being with Greg, and of how romantic he can be. Things were going wrong with Jeff. Yet no matter what was happening, Greg and I would remain in love.

Shortly after I returned from Zion, Jeff returned from camping. "There was a cliff next to my camp," Jeff excitedly told me after he parked his humming Mercedes and turned off the engine. "I was out walking last night and stumbled because it was dark. I almost fell over the cliff. I was concerned because I was carrying an ax. Then I realized that falling on the ax would not have been the main problem. The drop off was a hundred feet." He smiled as if he was happy to be alive. I was happy too.

At that moment, my mother called and said that her CD player was broken.

"I'll be right over," Jeff said.

He returned home with a grin, "I told Grandma that it would help if she plugged it in." Then he went to school.

After school, Jeff saved my mother from a scam. Her car mechanic had told her that she needed unnecessary repairs. Jeff had passed off his Utah *Safety Inspection Certification,* and came to her rescue. "Here's the handbook," he said. "See, they shouldn't be requiring that." Then Jeff called the mechanic who had tried to take advantage of my mother. In the face of Jeff's knowledge, the mechanic backed down.

On April 3, 2012 I met a man named Will at a Twelve Step Meeting. He had never walked due to a crippling birth defect. I learned that he had never used drugs or alcohol. His wife had kicked him out because of his weakness for porn. My instincts told me that he was a humble, sincere and good person. I believed him when he said he had quit using porn and was working on a permanent change of heart.

Maybe he can help with Jeff if we rent a room to him until his wife takes him back. Jeff is great with handicapped people, I smiled.

A few days later, my mother started driving on the wrong side of the road and got lost in our own neighborhood. A salesman came to her door and offered her a small amount of money for her car. She was about to be ripped off by him when I decided to buy her car for a fair price. I'd been praying for my brother Steve and his girlfriend in Oregon to get better transportation. His girlfriend's job of transporting elderly people was jeopardized by her old car's constant backfiring and stalling.

With Sandra watching over Jeff, I drove to Oregon to give my brother his car. Then, Steve drove me back to Utah, telling me about how he chased a bear out of the cabin where he lives—and about his neighbors shooting and killing each other.

"It's their fights over Meth!" Steve said. "Meth is really bad. Too many of my neighbors are crippled or dead because of it. If Meth doesn't kill them, then their gunfights will."

Steve was about to go home when he paused in the driveway and said, "Jeff is a real nice guy, but he's not serious about life. He's too interested in drugs and alcohol. I wanted to warn him, but what could I say? It took me forty years to quit my addictions. He'll have to learn like I did, by experience." Then Steve added, "All of the friends I grew up with who did drugs are dead, except the ones who quit."

Somehow, seeing my brother survive and express loving concern for Jeff was a buoy for my soul.

On April 9, 2012, I walked across the street to sit in the park and look at the results of an over-the-counter drug test I gave Jeff. Like a child, he was curious about the test, and brought me a urine sample willingly. Sitting in the park, I saw that the lines on the test proved he was on Meth. I reached for my phone to call probation. Then I realized I'd left my phone home, so I went to get it. To my surprise, probation was already there.

"Jeff, do you want to tell your mother what's going on?"

"No," he replied.

The officer looked at me. He had also given a drug test to Jeff. It was positive. "Jeff wants to spare you, but you should know I gave him an ultimatum—to be sent back to California to serve jail time, or to come up with some plan to show probation that he deserves another chance. He has until tomorrow to come up with a plan."

"Drug test me every week," Jeff told the probation officer.

Jeff was drug tested every Thursday. Unfortunately, that gave him the weekend to use Meth and then have it wear off before his next test.

Near the end of the school year, I rented a room in our condo to Will. Will was the man I met at the Twelve Step Meeting whose wife had kicked him out. He had been homeless and was glad to move in with his wheelchair until he and his wife reconciled. I trusted him to be a good friend to Jeff. Then, because tumor activity was affecting my brain, causing me memory loss, I went to California to take care of my health.

Jeff's probation officer said, "As long as Will stays in your condo, and Don and Lynn or Sandra check on Jeff, you can stay in California and leave Jeff here without you."

In my California backyard, my grandsons stopped playing with their cars in the dirt and ran up to me. I hugged them and smiled, thinking of the weekend to come.

All my children and grandchildren would be together for a family reunion. Jeff and his six siblings would sleep under the same roof for the first time in fifteen years. Eli's wife and my daughter Christy selected a beautiful vacation house near Zion National Park so that Jeff would be able to attend without missing school. We named the house, "Our Zion House."

I hugged my grandsons again as a breeze teased my hair. Sunbeams sparkled on dew covered grass. Birds sang in the trees. The beauty surrounding me took my breath away. I was saying goodbye to California for what I hoped was the last time. I would visit Utah for our family reunion and then move home to California for good.

May 19, 2012: Jeff slept through the first day of our family reunion while the grandchildren played outside. *Jeff's probably tired from working on diesel trucks at school in 100 degree temperatures,* I said to myself—hoping it wasn't drugs.

The next day, we hiked down a hill beside our Zion House, to explore the canyon below. Jeff and Tim became animated, and began reminiscing their past.

"Remember the time my car went over the cliff and stuck on a tree root?" Tim asked his twin.

"Yeah. That root kept your car from plunging into the canyon," Jeff said, as he carried Tim's son Orion on his shoulders. "After we crawled out of the back window and up that tree, your car was still in perfect condition. If only that tow truck hadn't flipped it upside down while pulling it out."

Eli's wife was shocked—being new to the family and the antics of her brothers-in-law. She looked at Eli questioningly. Yet, before he could explain, Tim dug up another memory.

"Remember the time we found some sleeping cows in the hills and tried to push them over?"

"Yeah," Jeff replied. "You said it's easy to push a cow over when it's asleep, but we couldn't—no matter how hard we tried!"

Tim laughed a hearty laugh before reminiscing, "Remember the time Mom and Dad were gone and we borrowed their car to go to the lake?"

"I warned you," Jeff said, "that Dad would check the odometer and we shouldn't drive so far."

"Yeah," Tim replied, "but I had fun driving the car backwards on the way home, to take the mileage off."

Jeff looked sheepish, and we all started laughing. Except Greg, who asked, "How many times did you borrow our car while we were gone?"

They smiled at each other and Tim replied, "You don't want to know."

During our hike, Tim and Jeff continued reminiscing their younger days—like the time they discharged our fire extinguishers just for the thrill of it—and the time they threw our spare light bulbs onto the street just to hear them pop!

I'd forgotten about their childhood mischief.

At the bottom of the canyon, my family played in the stream while I laid down under a shady ledge and fell asleep. I awoke to a cool breeze on my face and saw Greg waiting for me. The rest of our family had left for the house. Greg and I began hiking out of the canyon.

"Tim's out of the forest now," Greg said. "Yet Jeff has a long way to go. I'm pretty sure it was a hangover that caused him to sleep all day yesterday. I checked out several rehabs for Jeff to go to after his graduation next month, but none of them take autistic persons."

I looked at Greg and gently said, "I have a dream of creating a homemade rehab for Jeff on one of the Channel Islands. It could be for nine weeks—one week for each person in our family to spend time with him. If he needs love, he'll get it, one on one with each of us. Unitedly, our family love could heal him—or so it seems in my dreams."

"I've heard of that before," Greg replied, "people getting sober by going off to live in a cave or in a wilderness somewhere. That would be great if you could talk Jeff into it."

Tuesday, May 22, 2012, St. George: Our family reunion was like a safe bubble for Jeff—with hiking, swimming, exploring and eating together as a family. Most outstanding was the annular solar eclipse which only comes every few hundred years in any particular part of the world. Together we watched the eclipsing of the sun form slivery shadows on our faces, hands, arms, and shirts. We looked at each other in awe. On the ground, the slivery patterns turned the world into a configuration of light and dark shapes everywhere we looked.

That night, we sat around the fire pit and talked for hours under the stars. Matt and Jeff were the last to watch the embers die.

The reunion ended and our mountain utopia came to a close. Jeff returned to St. George and immediately drove off in his car with his friends. I could hear one of the passengers singing a song about pot as they pulled out of the driveway.

Later that day, I ran an errand and stopped at a red light. Jeff's Mercedes pulled up beside me, with Jeff behind the wheel. Scraggly looking people hung out of the windows with their cigarettes. They cheered when they saw me.

"Hey! It's Jeff's Mom! How good to see you!" they beamed.

I would have been flattered that I was so popular, but Jeff's life was going downhill and I was mad at his friends. When I first met them, I showed them love and respect. This time I did not even force a smile.

Later, Jeff returned home to our condo. All I could think of doing before he left again was to suggest that we pray. With a loving tone, Jeff said a tender prayer: *Thanks for cars, friends, and this pretty world.*

After praying he said, "I love you." Then he left.

God, he is yours, I whispered.

CHAPTER SIXTEEN

I made an appointment to see Jeff's probation officer. "Jeff needs another rehab," I explained. "I want to use one of the islands off the coast of California. Santa Rosa Island has no stores on it, so there will be no liquor. It's in the chain of islands that Jeff used to sail to with his twin brother."

"A vacation won't help," the officer said. "When Jeff returns from the island, he'll go back to his old ways. He's not going to make it. He has two dirty drug tests already."

I refused to give in, saying, "The island will be my last chance to be with Jeff before we split paths: him living in Utah and me in California. I'd like one more happy memory with Jeff."

I waited for the officer's reply. Neither of us moved. Finally he said, "Even though I don't think it will help, I'll give you a travel permit." He handed me a permit, then wrote down the number of a sober living house, saying, "This is in case you need it when Jeff comes back. Good luck."

That afternoon I showed Jeff his travel permit for going to Santa Rosa Island.

"I'm not going," Jeff said. Then he walked out the door and rode away on his motorcycle. It was his first day of summer break from Dixie Technical College's Diesel Engine Program.

Two days later, Jeff returned and leaned against the wall of our front porch. "I fell off my motorcycle and think I broke a bone," he said with pain written all over his face. He limped inside, eased himself down on the couch, and showed me a purple bruise that covered his thigh.

Jeff didn't move for the rest of the day. From the couch, he watched me pack supplies into backpacks. "This is enough food to last a month," I said.

"I'm not going to the island," he replied.

"If you don't go, I'll go alone and fill up the ocean with my tears," I told him. "The island will be our last chance to be together. I won't be living in Utah anymore," I reminded him as he stared off into space, sadly.

That evening, James drove to Saint George on his way to Glacier National Park where he, Matt, and Phil had summer jobs. James fixed two plates of tacos for himself and Jeff. Then he sat beside Jeff to eat. I sat on the floor in front of the couch and handed James a pamphlet that Jeff had earlier refused to look at. James took the pamphlet and began to read:

Santa Rosa Island is 45 miles offshore.

It has 55 miles of coastline, white sand beaches, tide pools, canyons, wildflowers, sand carvings, archeology, fossils, rolling grasslands, oak groves and the rare Torrey Pine.

Some of the animals on the island are the red fox, deer, elk, and horses, with the humpback whale nearby.

The temperature in May averages 50 degrees.

Strong winds.

Bring extra food in case weather cancels departure from the island.

Precautions: Deaths occur from falling off cliffs and swimming.

James turned to Jeff and said, "I've heard that the red fox on Santa Rosa Island is found nowhere else in the world."

Jeff finished eating his tacos and asked, "What if my bone has a fracture? Walking on the island would be bad for my leg."

"I'll call a doctor," I said.

An x-ray showed his bone wasn't broken.

"I'm not worried about my leg anymore," Jeff said. "What are we waiting for? Let's go."

During the night Greg drove us to a small airport in Camarillo and chartered a Cessna for our flight. We loaded our gear and said goodbye to Greg. Surrounded by a soft ocean breeze we climbed aboard with the two pilots. Soon we were gazing down from the sky at an aqua sea and white foam crests. "It's beautiful," I mouthed to Jeff against the roar of the engine. He nodded in agreement.

We passed over Anacapa Island's green mountain meadows. Then, over Santa Cruz Island, I looked down and saw frothy waves smack the steep cliffs. Approaching Santa Rosa Island, I felt peace bear up my heart before our plane touched the dirt runway.

After we landed, the pilot said, "You get the whole campground to yourselves. No boats are chartered to come for over a month. The ranger station is three miles up the road."

I took a deep breath. This was it. A wilderness rehab for Jeff and me.

"Water Canyon Campground is on the other side of that hill," the pilot said, pointing south.

Jeff led the way, limping through a field of orange and white wild flowers that rippled in the wind as we crested the hill. The valley below was a breathtaking sight of green grasses surrounded by canyon streams and cliffs.

Jeff set up his camp beside a deep canyon. I set up my camp a football field's length away from Jeff's camp, beside the restroom with solar-heated showers. We made a camp in between for cooking. Shortly after, a ranger dropped by and said, "You won't last here more than three days. The last campers didn't. The wind blew their tents down the canyon into the river. Let me know if you want me to wire the airport to send someone to pick you up."

The wind had already whipped sand into our faces, but compared to the havoc of Jeff's crystal meth and alcohol use, the wind was easy.

During the night, I tried to keep the sand out of my eyes and the grit out of my teeth. The ranger had insinuated that we were wimps, which fueled my determination to endure the wind without complaint. Then, during the night, the temperature dropped and the island suddenly became still. My imagination got the better of me. I feared a monstrous storm was coming, like in the book, *The Cay,* where islanders tied themselves to palm trees while a storm sandblasted them so harshly that their clothing was torn off and their skin bloodied.

I got up, walked to a ridge, and searched the sky. An orange-ish glow lay between the stars and the sea and I feared it was the sign of a hurricane coming. I imagined Jeff's tent being blown into the canyon, and me going down to rescue him after the storm. I finally lied back down in my sleeping bag and took deep, relaxing breaths until I fell asleep. The storm never came. Funny how fears float away as quickly as they come.

The next morning, I gazed at the sea which had a silver lining. A meadowlark sang as sunlight began dancing like bouncing diamonds on the water. The grasses bent in a gentle breeze as Jeff walked by and said, "Hi Mom." His voice sent power through me.

Later, I rested on the grass while Jeff cooked rice, raisins, and cashews with fresh lime juice. We ate by the canyon stream with water as smooth as a mirror except where tiny ripples danced around the cattails. In the distance, Santa Cruz Island posed between the canyon walls like a framed painting.

We were living in a timeless paradise with no clocks except for the sun and the moon.

One day, Jeff walked along the ocean and I hiked to the Torrey Pines. The pine needles were flat, like beaver tails. The mulch was so deep that I couldn't find the bottom when I poked a stick into the ground. These rare pines are found only in one other place in the world, on the coast of San Diego.

That evening, Jeff walked into camp with news that made my heart stand still. He approached me with a smile and then turned serious, "By the ocean I jumped between two cliffs and slipped. I caught myself between the ledges. If I fell further, there would have been no way for me to get out and no one would have known where I was. I hung onto the ledge with my fingernails. I put my toes in a crack in the rock and I climbed out."

Tears came to my eyes, and a lump in my throat, as I thought of how many times I almost lost him, since his premature birth over 30 years ago.

The next day, Jeff and I walked in opposite directions on the shore exploring caves only accessible during low tide. Then back together again, we made sandcastles decorated with shells, sticks and colorful stones. Jeff watched a fuzzy caterpillar crawl on the white sand and picked it up. He gently placed it on a bush away from the water. Then he announced, "As long as I'm here, I may as well swim in the ocean."

I watched him walk into the sea and dive beneath the waves. Suddenly there appeared a black ball next to him and I realized that Jeff wasn't swimming alone. A seal with a shiny round head was following him. When Jeff finished his swim, he stood up in shallow water, looked back, and saw the seal watching him. With a smile, he said, "Oh, I have a friend."

The next week, at the crack of dawn, Jeff and I began hiking up Lobo Canyon. A stream of water ran beside us and reeds with black and green stripes brushed against our legs. Polliwogs swam amongst colorful rocks. In the trees moss hung, resembling Christmas garlands swaying in the breeze. Jeff walked ahead in silence into grass as high as his chest.

Suddenly, he stopped, broke off a piece of grass, cupped his hands around it, blew into his hands. The noise that he made was like honking geese. I broke off a piece of grass and did the same. Then we followed the trail to an arch that looked like a giant clam. We stood in the arch and gazed at the canyon. Intricate shapes reminded me of scenes from the Grand Canyon, Zion National Park, the hills back home, and the TV show *Lost in Space.* The wind whistled in graduating pitches through dozens of small canyons merging onto our trail.

The next thing I knew, Jeff was so far ahead of me that I walked alone for an hour, unafraid of predators. On Santa Rosa Island there are no predators.

At the end of Lobo Canyon I stepped onto a lava rock. Jeff was perched on a plateau taking pictures. I walked up to him as the surf crashed and the stones rumbled. He pointed out a distant ship at sea. In silence, we sat and watched.

That evening, we walked out of the canyon under a rose-colored sky. Stars came out before I reached the camp where I found Jeff adding salt and pepper to almonds frying in olive oil. I ate several handfuls of his delicious treat and went to bed. Before dozing off, I saw Jeff walking over to me. He asked, "Would you like to look at my pictures?" I envisioned photographs of rock formations, catapulting waves, white sand beaches, and millions of sparkling water droplets exploding through the air.

I said, "Yes." He showed me his photos. They were all of the distant ship at sea.

Our last night on the island, I handed Jeff El Libro, inviting him to open to any page. He opened and read, "God hath called us to peace. He that is called of the Lord is the Lord's freeman."

As he closed the book, I thought of the addictions enslaving him. Suddenly, a mockingbird began to sing, waves broke on a distant shore, a seal barked, and a frog chorus filled the air. Then a clap sounded—like thunder—as a wave exploded on the beach, silencing the frog chorus.

Slowly, the moon peeked over the east ridge of the canyon and the frogs resumed their opus. I fell asleep. Then, just before sunrise, I woke up and saw three falling stars. I smiled and made a wish for Jeff's recovery.

CHAPTER SEVENTEEN

Our flight to the mainland felt magical as we soared over scores of fishing boats. I had only one regret: Our island paradise came to an end before anyone else in our family came to camp with us. Phil had wanted to join us, but with no phone reception on the island, our communication was blocked.

I saw Greg by the airstrip when the Cessna landed. I ran across the runway into his arms. He'd granted Jeff and me a heavenly retreat—an escape from the pains we knew. Soon Greg would arrange my surgery for my tumors. But first we needed to take Jeff to Utah.

After conferring with Greg, I told Jeff, "We're not going to our condo until you interview at a sober house. I'm afraid you'll get too comfortable at our condo and delay your sober living."

Jeff replied, "I'll call the sober house tomorrow." Then he got that look of wanting drugs, and our trip to Utah became a nightmare.

I called the sober house before we left California. I was anxious to make arrangements before our arrival in St. George.

"I'm calling to see if you have any openings," I told the director.

The director abruptly replied, "You have ruined your son's chance of getting into my sober house. He is supposed to call, not you."

"He plans to call tomorrow," I said, adding that he is autistic and slow in handling social interactions.

"If your son is that handicapped, we don't want him," the director said. "The reason he's got a problem is because of you. He can't get better if you are helping him. He has to do it on his own."

I sank to my knees, my heart pounding in my chest, and said, "I'm sorry. I didn't mean to ruin it for him. I won't call anymore. Please talk to my son when he calls." I sobbed when I hung up, my whole body shaking. The words echoed in my head: *You have ruined your son's chance.* I found peace, thinking, *God is in charge. I just need faith.*

The next morning Jeff called the director of the sober living house. He was refused.

We checked into a hotel in St. George to wait for Jeff to find a sober house. "There are other sober living houses," I told him as he finished unloading some luggage into our hotel room. "Surely you can find one before your father and I have to go back to California."

The next thing I knew, Greg and Jeff were walking toward the grocery store. Shortly after, Greg returned alone with a troubled look on his face. He said, "As we rounded a corner, Jeff disappeared, saying he had to go somewhere. I waited for him to come back, but he didn't."

The next day Jeff called. "I-I-I spent the night at some-some-someone's house. I ju-just didn't want-want you-you t-to worry about me," he said, with loud voices laughing in the background.

Later, I called Jeff's number and a girl answered, saying, "Your son is letting me use his phone and he doesn't want to talk to you right now."

Greg and I saw no sense in waiting around. We drove back to California with Jeff on the loose and with our friend Will—in his wheelchair—guarding our condo.

When I called probation to tell them that Jeff was living in an undisclosed place the officer said, "I just saw Jeff. He came in for his regular appointment."

Jeff is more responsible than I thought, I smiled.

The next week, Will called, saying "Jeff came back to the condo. I know he is not allowed. What should I do?"

"Act calm and don't agitate him," I replied. I pictured Jeff walking down the hallway while coming off Meth and being unable to get past Will's wheelchair. In my imagination I saw Jeff pick up the wheelchair with Will in it and toss it aside, the way he had thrown the bicycle through our living room window when he tripped over it.

The next day Will called again, saying, "I found a bottle of pickles shattered on the kitchen floor. My wheelchair will track the pickle juice everywhere and I can't get out of my chair to clean up the mess."

I remembered the half gallon bottle of pickles left over from our family reunion. I had hoped for Will to be a calming influence on Jeff—that Jeff wouldn't throw things. But my hopes were dashed. I grabbed my purse and shoes. I called my landlord to arrange for a quick move out. Then, with a rush of adrenaline, I drove to Utah.

In the meantime, Will's wife decided that she was ready to end their separation and Will had a happy reunion with his family.

When I arrived at my condo, I found Lynn and her husband Don at my house with Jeff. "We stopped by and saw Jeff cleaning up some pickles that spilled on your floor," they said. I was amazed to see the kitchen floor shiny and clean.

I turned to Jeff and said, "Will you help me clean up the rest of the condo? I've arranged to return the keys to my landlord in two days." Jeff agreed.

Then Lynn said, "If Jeff doesn't find a place to live by then, he can stay with us."

Lynn and Don had sold their ranch and were living in a beautiful home in St. George.

Jeff would be staying in the home of Lynn and her husband Don, a retired California Highway Patrolman. I was elated!

Jeff and I prepared to move out of our condo. Jeff got rid of the surplus engines in our garage. He built a pond in Lynn and Don's backyard for his fish and turtles to go in. Then he drained the water out of our backyard pond at the request of our landlord. We took the turkey out of our freezer and cooked it for a goodbye party. Sandra came to help. We invited all of our friends and family to come and eat and take things which we needed to give away.

The next evening, our turkey dinner was an affectionate gathering, with the love of family and friends. Jeff was happy to eat and relax after working hard. He gave his aquarium to his cousins. They were delighted!

The next day, we watered our vegetable garden for the last time. When our landlord arrived for her inspection she asked, "Did you follow my directions and take out your garden?" She had wanted the backyard leveled to dirt for the new renters—like it was when we moved in. We led her outside and showed her the sign we made.

Welcome to Our Garden:
Carrots, Spinach, Columbines, Swiss Chard,
Tomatoes, Squash and Onions.

"We didn't have the heart to murder our plants," I told her.

She stared at our plants for a minute, and then asked, "How often do the plants need to be watered?"

"Daily," I replied as I handed her our keys, and we said goodbye to the condo, hoping the vegetables would survive to bless someone else.

I stored my furniture in my mom's garage and returned to California. The next week, I returned to St. George to get the furniture. But my tumors were causing such head pain that I accidentally knocked off some of my mom's roof with my U-haul rental truck. Jeff came to my rescue and drove the truck home to California for me.

When we arrived in Simi, Jeff walked into the hills looking his best, in a Hawaiian shirt. At first, he returned as handsome as ever, and said, "I couldn't find anybody in the hills." *An answer to my prayers.*

The next day, he disappeared and when he returned, he had no shirt, no shoes, torn pants, and a red sweaty face. He was on Meth. He got on our computer at midnight and something whispered to my heart, *It's better he hurt the computer than you.*

I was frightened over Jeff's state of mind—especially with my grandchildren living in the house. So I put the dog in the car and invited

Jeff to go back to Utah. We drove all night, with Jonny dog on Jeff's lap. I poured 8 bottles of water on my head to keep me awake. Then I checked into a St. George hotel and Jeff went to Lynn and Don's house.

At the hotel with my dog, I convalesced while Greg arranged for my tumor removal in Florida in the best clinic in the world for the type of tumors I had. Then, the next day, Greg mentioned on the phone that the computer quit working the night Jeff left. I gave Jeff a call.

"I put the hard drive in the glove box of our car," he said, "because I was mad about leaving California."

That night I accepted a dinner invitation from Lynn and Don. I watched a sober Jeff place corn on the cob on their barbeque beside the best steak I'd ever tasted. Then Jeff showed me an enchanting aviary he built for Lynn—filled with cockatiels, parakeets, finches and stained-glass murals of birds.

After dinner, Lynn led me into their living room. I felt like a child at Christmas. Bright colors were everywhere on the walls, couches and floors. Colored lights streamed through lamps shaped like birds, fish and dragons. "Jeff likes it here," Lynn said. "We decided to let him stay with us indefinitely."

Greg caught a ride to Utah with a friend and drove me home. Sandra handled Jeff's disability money, checking receipts and taking him shopping.

Once, Sandra told me on the phone, "Jeff put a rubber ducky on the hood of his Mercedes-Benz. I told him people might think it looks funny, but he keeps it there anyway."

I didn't know whether to laugh or cry over Jeff's mix of autism and addiction which made him eccentric.

Later that summer my tumors were removed, and I settled into life without Jeff. However, memories continued to float through my heart of our days together when he was the class genius, raising hundreds of tropical fish, and reading verses with me like:

Love suffers long,
And is kind.
Love does not envy.

Love does not think itself better than another.
Love is not prideful.
Love is not selfish.
Love bears all things, believes all things,
Hopes all things, and endures all things.
Love lasts forever.

Chapter Eighteen

"My Mercedes broke down," Jeff said. "I'm in California."

In alarm, I asked, "Why are you coming to California? Did you get a travel permit?"

"No, but I'm in California—at the Cajon Pass. And my car broke down," he replied.

"You need permission from your probation officer to leave Utah. I'll be there as soon as I can make it," I replied, planning to drive to the pass and take him back to Utah where he belonged.

When I got to the pass, a few hours later, I parked my van next to Jeff's Mercedes which was parked in an empty lot. It was a cold day and all the windows were rolled down. Jeff was leaning back in the front seat of his car without a shirt. His hair was knotted. His clothes were greasy. Yet what alarmed me most was the expression on his face—it was hard.

Suddenly he handed me a shoe box from the inside of his car.

"Look inside," he said without a smile.

I didn't trust him. Thoughts of rattlesnakes, rats, and poisonous bugs crossed through my mind. I handed it back.

Jeff took the box and opened it. "How do you like my centipede?" he asked. "Can we get a cage for it when we get back to Simi Valley?"

Despite his inebriation, he softened my heart. Memories flashed through my mind of all the insects and animals he's loved. There flashed through my mind a memory of him kneeling on the desert floor to smell a cactus flower. *He loves small and innocent things, maybe because he, in a way, is like a small and innocent child himself.*

We began the 330 mile drive to St. George with Jeff in the passenger seat of my van. The penalty for leaving the state of Utah without permission from his probation officer would land him in jail. I had no trouble staying awake at the wheel.

When we stopped for gas in Barstow, Jeff asked for cigarettes. I bought him some—which I'd never done before. He was agitated and I reasoned, *At least he won't get inebriated from smoking.* Then we stopped for gas in Las Vegas and Jeff asked for a beer. I bought him juice instead.

I drove back onto the freeway as Jeff drank his juice. When he finished, he rolled down the window and threw the empty juice container out of the van. He was agitated. *We're only a hundred miles from St. George,* I said to myself.

"What would you do if I broke the windshield?" Jeff asked casually.

"I'd keep driving," I said, hoping a calm answer wouldn't rile him.

Then, through the corner of my eye I saw Jeff raise his foot. Suddenly, a crash sounded from the impact of Jeff's boot hitting the windshield.

"Oh Lord," I cried, praying for God to hold me when I saw the cracked window. Then I stared at the road ahead, and continued driving.

Jeff bowed his head in shame as sunlight glimmered through the cracks of a hundred ripples in the windshield.

I took Jeff to Lynn and Don's house. As he got out of my van he said, "I got kicked out of Utah by my probation officer. I'm supposed to be in California."

I had just transported my son to the wrong state.

"I need a break," I told Lynn as I began backing out of her driveway.

Lynn replied, "He gave us no notice that he was leaving and he left all his stuff here. It's good that Jeff is back, even if just for a few days."

Jeff stood beside Lynn and said, "I should kill my Mom for taking me back to Utah." Lynn came unglued and told me to leave quickly.

I was angry, and disowned my son. I reasoned that this book about his life was coming to a sad ending. In my imagination, I pictured myself standing by his grave reminiscing on a life snuffed out by drugs.

I parked near a red rock mountain, despondent and numb. After a while, I lifted my eyes to look up. The sky cast a reddish glow over me. As I watched, a crimson red sunset spread across the entire sky like flames. Moved to tears by the beauty, my numb feelings woke up and I sobbed.

I need help, I whispered. I drove to the Visitor's Center of the St. George Temple, walked in, and asked one of the workers there for a blessing for the sick. The sympathetic man laid his hands on my head and gave me a sweet, tender blessing. A power of love greater than my own began to lift me up. I called Greg and said, "I feel forgiveness. God has a way of changing everything."

"Yes, God is in charge," Greg said, "and we must have faith."

My love for Greg deepened.

I slept at Sandra's house. She sat down beside me the next day, saying, "You've done all you can. There's nothing left to do but give him to God. That's what my mother did with me when I went through my wild years."

The next morning, I called Jeff's probation officer. He told me that Jeff was caught with alcohol—his third violation of parole. "He has to leave the state," the officer said. "But I didn't think he'd leave so fast without telling anyone."

Then Lynn called me, saying, "We're having a garage sale and Jeff sold his turquoise motorcycle to pay for your broken windshield."

I'd watched him paint that motorcycle his favorite color, back while we lived in our condo. That motorcycle was the one that Jeff fixed up for his welding class. I went to Lynn's house and Jeff gave me the money.

After my windshield was replaced, Jeff called and asked, "Can I take you out to Nielsen's Frozen Custard?"

If it had been a day earlier, I would have said no. But my windshield was fixed, Jeff had sobered up, and my heart felt soft. "Yes," I replied.

I picked Jeff up in Lynn's driveway and he said, "I have no money, can you buy our frozen custard?"

"Yes," I replied with a smile.

We sat in Nielsen's, silently eating Frozen Bumbleberry Custard and Caramel Cashew Custard. When we finished, Jeff confided, "The California court might give me six months in jail." I hoped it would be long enough to cure his addiction.

Jeff and I left for California. He never graduated from college—he missed an exam during our family reunion and never made it up. Yet I felt love in my heart, and I had a new windshield.

Suddenly a truck drove by, kicked up a rock, and Bang! My windshield was cracked!

Jeff laughed out loud. "It's not always my fault that your windshield gets cracked," he said.

We checked into a motel at the Cajon Pass near his car. I noticed the rubber duck was still on the Mercedes hood.

The next day was Sunday and Jeff rode with me to a church by the motel. He sat patiently in the parking lot while I went inside to recharge my heart. Then Jeff and I took a side road through the mountains to look at lakes and streams. In our motel room, later that night, Jeff watched television with no sound—so he wouldn't disturb me. Our time together was sweet. I picked up a diary that James gave me for my birthday. I was saving it for a special time. A quote on the cover made me think of Jeff:

See how nature,
Trees, flowers and grass,
Grow in silence.
See the stars, the moon and the sun,
How they move in silence.
...we need silence to be able to touch souls.
—Mother Teresa

Before leaving Cajon Pass, Jeff called his brother Phil. "I'm worried about my pet centipede. While I'm in jail, will you take care of it?" he asked. Phil said, "Yes."

After they talked, Jeff started his Mercedes with jumper cables and we drove our cars to Simi Valley.

I saw a sign beside the road that said, *Expect Miracles*. A miracle was happening in my heart. I remembered a quote that someone said at church:

You learn the most from your hardest child.

Jeff was proving that to be true. And what I was learning—above all else—was love.

On our way to Simi Valley, Jeff's centipede died. He made plans to give it a funeral in the hills before going to jail.

CHAPTER NINETEEN

Jeff's court date—for violating probation—was scheduled for a month away, in December. So Jeff went to the hills. My heart broke as we said goodbye. Before he left, he paused to say, "I'd still like to see you and Dad. Maybe we can go out for ice cream when I get out of jail." Then his car disappeared, and I knew he would not be the same the next time I saw him.

God be with you, I whispered as I felt my heart go numb. I wanted to call Butterfly, but grief immobilized me.

Suddenly my phone rang.

"My butt says you need some help," Butterfly announced.

I was amazed! Even though she said it in a cheeky way, my prayer for help was answered! I poured out my heart about my shattered dreams for Jeff. Then added, "In his car are his college books, his birth certificate and more. He'll lose it all."

To my delight, the next day Jeff came home. He dropped off his birth certificate, books, awards, and sentimental stuff.

Jeff parked his Mercedes in a dry riverbed where someone stole his tires, battery, other car parts and broke the windows. Jeff set a match to the gas tank—after removing his rubber duck and placing it safely in a tree. Then he watched the car go up in flames. That night, he was arrested for drug-related charges. He could have been arrested for arson, but the police decided not to cite him for burning his own car.

Repeatedly Jeff went to jail for public intoxication while awaiting his arraignment for violating probation. During one of our visits in jail, he said with a smile, "I planted flowers in the trunk of my Mercedes, in its resting place. I water the flowers every time I get out of jail."

During one of our jail visits I told Jeff that his disability money was off limits until he was sober.

"Leave!" Jeff yelled, "Go!" He was angry as he backed away from me and went to the door.

I was glad that he used only his voice to express himself and threw no chair and hit no glass. I lay in my van in the jail parking lot, remembering an acronym I made up after reading a book by Phil A. Hughes. Phil wrote about a child whose mother never smiled, and whose dad threw her across the room breaking her leg. In foster care, the child did the only thing she'd learned how to do, and that was to act like her parents. It was only through using *P.L.A.C.E. (Play, Love, Acceptance, Curiosity, and Empathy)* that the foster parent could help the child connect with people. I was thinking about practicing those traits with my family, when my phone rang.

"I called to say I'm sorry for getting mad," Jeff said from the jail phone, his tender voice touching my heart.

When Jeff was due to be released from jail, I waited in the jail lobby to take him home. Yet I had a problem—Greg didn't want Jeff to come home. Greg wasn't ignorant of the fact that Jeff recently broke my windshield. I'd set up a separate living space for Jeff at one end of our home—with no access to the rest of the house. I called it Safe Haven, a sober house. Yet Greg said No to Jeff coming home. While I waited for Jeff's release, I wondered where I would take him. As I prayed for answers, a plumbing leak in the jail postponed Jeff's release.

I picked up my phone and made a call. "Can Jeff and I spend the night?" I asked Greg's brother who taught drug rehabilitation.

"I'd let you stay the night, but I have to go to work early in the morning," he said.

I asked a friend who was picking up her daughter from jail if she could house me and Jeff for the night. Jeff had been sober for several weeks in jail. She said No.

Then I called my best girlfriend Claire in Oregon. When she picked up the phone, I started crying, "I'm picking up Jeff from jail and don't have any place to go. Greg says I can't bring him home and for the first time I'm not angry at Greg for saying no. I just love him. Yet I feel lost with nowhere to go."

Claire said she'd pray for Greg to let Jeff come home.

At that moment Jeff walked out. He was happy to see me. I hung up the phone and asked, "Where do you want to eat?"

"How about Wendy's?" he asked.

"Sounds like a plan," I said, relieved that I didn't have to tell him yet that we had nowhere to go.

We got in the car and I began backing out of the jail parking lot, when my phone rang. It was Greg. "I talked to Tim," Greg said. "He said it should be fine to let Jeff come back home if he agrees not to use drugs or alcohol." At the time, Tim had a wife and two young children living at our house, yet he was willing to give Jeff a chance.

I felt joy! For the first time, we had our own sober house, Safe Haven for Jeff to live in.

Jeff stayed home for several days. He changed my van's oil, pulled up a passion fruit vine that was strangling our garden, and made plans to put up new fencing in our yard. His Kentucky nieces sent him loving text messages. And, as always, he showed me boats on the internet.

I read about sober living houses on the computer. I read about giving drug tests, having the addict earn privileges, and most importantly, the first rule was: DO NOT GIVE THEM MONEY. The second rule was: DO NOT GIVE THEM MONEY. The third rule was: DO NOT GIVE THEM MONEY.

Over time, Jeff was in and out of Safe Haven. I drug and alcohol tested him before giving him a room. If he hadn't earned the privilege to come inside, I let him take cold showers with our garden house, out behind our shed.

On November 25, 2012 Jeff left Safe Haven to go to the hills. On December 13 he went to court for his sentencing for violating probation.

Greg and I drove to court and saw Jeff walk in smelling like alcohol. He wore no shoes and had a baby blanket on his head—it had a dog face with floppy ears on it. His hair stuck out from underneath and was ratted in knots. His clothes were dirty. In my diary I wrote: *He's standing in front of the judge now. One would think he was trying to dress like a mentally ill person on purpose to get sympathy. But knowing him, it's no act.*

The judge, prosecutor, and defender huddle like a team fighting for the same goal—to help Jeff. Their hearts are drawn out to him, as if to a child. I pray while they deliberate in their huddle.

"Jeff must serve 15 days in Ventura County Jail—starting on December 26, 2012," the judge said. Then she added, "He will no more be on parole."

Fifteen days! Not the predicted 6 months! And no parole means that he'll be free to leave the state if I want to take him back to Utah!

Jeff was supposed to turn himself into jail on December 26, but he did not even come home for Christmas. He was sick in a tent in the hills.

On New Years Day 2013, some police came and Jeff called out from his tent, "Hey, I'm glad to see you! I'm supposed to go to jail. Can you give me a ride?"

They put him in their police car, which then got stuck in the mud. While they were spinning their wheels to get out, the car caught on fire. Jeff told me about it when I visited him in jail.

"I knew I could have gotten the police car out of the mud if they would have let me behind the wheel, but I was handcuffed in the back seat. They kept spinning the tires. The catalytic converter was overheating. Sparks from the converter started the fire. It will probably cost a thousand dollars to fix the damage."

I smiled over the irony. All of Jeff's life he's helped others get their cars out of the mud. If the police would only have let him get behind the wheel, he would have gotten their car unstuck before it caught fire. But Jeff patiently sat in the back of the police car as a silent observer.

About that time, Matt, now 20-years-old, moved back home after renting his own apartment. To my delight, he vowed to live sober, or sleep outdoors with the dog. Like Jeff, he had a weakness for alcohol, but he wanted to do something with his life. He offered to pay rent and turn over a new leaf.

James had also moved out, but when he saw how well Matt was doing he knocked on our front door and asked, "Can I rent a space under your apple tree for my tent? I've adopted a Henry Thoreau lifestyle while attending college. I rented land from a farmer and put my tent there. I go to the gym to take my showers."

"You can live here inside the house," I replied. Yet James insisted on a tent by the apple tree. He gave up his earthly possessions for a back-to-nature experience.

Next, Phil saw how happy everyone was and asked if he could move home too. Greg and I said, "Yes." Our time together with our three youngest boys living at home, along with Tim's family, was a blissful season I will never forget.

On February 24, 2013 Jeff came to our home and knocked on the door at 2:30 AM. Phil was up playing his guitar. He woke me, and I stepped out on the porch. I saw Jeff sitting on our bench. His jeans were ripped into shreds below his knees and his knees were lacerated. He had a large patch of raw skin on his hip—red and oozing—where he skidded on his side after his bike crashed. I was holding back tears when I noticed that he had shoes on. Not the same ones as when I last saw him, but at least he had shoes. I was happy that he could at least walk and talk.

He tested 0% for alcohol, but the drug test showed that he was on pot and Meth so I gave him some socks, one of my large sweat shirts, a purple beanie that my grandkids gave me, and sent him on his way. Phil resumed playing his guitar—a beautiful song about searching for love, as Jeff disappeared into the night.

That Spring, I housed Jeff when he came home sober. When he was inebriated, he occasionally dropped by just to say Hi.

Then, one day I bought him a little moped, and took him back to St. George where he signed up for classes at Dixie Tech. Jeff's former teacher was happy to have his class genius back.

I found a place for Jeff to stay in St. George while he attended his first day of school. It was with a security guard named Dave, who looked like Santa Claus, and his kind wife who was a nurse. It was easy to find these nice people because our friends from church knew them.

I met Jeff after school. He looked happy, as he walked out of class with another student, and a big smile on his face.

I left Jeff at Dave's house, thinking, *He will graduate in three months if all goes well.* But a week later I got a call from his teacher, saying, "Jeff came to school intoxicated when I had a substitute teacher filling for me. He pulled out a vodka bottle in the middle of class." Then with a choked-up voice Jeff's teacher said, "Jeff was the most gifted student I've ever had. Some of the students tried to talk to him and help him, but Jeff told them, 'I've been this way most of my life. I'm not going to change.' I'm so sorry to inform you that Jeff was expelled. Maybe Jeff should go to another rehab before he tries to finish school."

I talked on the phone to Jeff's landlord Dave. "Now that Jeff's kicked out of school, he's started working odd jobs in town," Dave said.

Later, Dave called, saying, "I had to tackle Jeff and hold him down to get him to quit throwing a knife against the wall. I tried to talk him into going to a rehab. I care about him a lot, but he appears to be on Meth. I asked him to leave until he's sober—or I'd call the police."

I was amazed at how Dave stayed in control.

The next day, Jeff went to Dave's house and asked Dave to buy him a beer. When Dave refused, Jeff walked out and burned his college books in Dave's BBQ, then left.

That night I asked my grandchildren to pray for Jeff. Shortly after, he was arrested for eight violations while riding his moped: no tags; an unsafe lane change; didn't stop for the police at first; resisted arrest by arguing; no proof of registration, insurance, or license; and in the backpack he wore while driving his moped was a bottle of alcohol that had been partly drunk.

We had been praying for Jeff to let Dave take him to rehab. But instead, Jeff made his first trip to *Purgatory*—a Utah jail next to the DMV where Jeff got his driver's license and registered his Mercedes a year ago.

Jeff's arrest was an answer to my prayer—it stopped his substance abuse.

I remembered reading about some boys in a war-torn country. They had been kidnapped by military leaders who killed the boys' families, gave the boys drugs, and turned them into killers who burned down schools and murdered children. When the war ended, the boys were put in a drug rehab. A few of the men running the rehab got their bones busted by the boys, but they stuck it out and reformed them, giving them a chance for a better life. If those boys could be reformed, I reasoned, so could Jeff.

June 2013: I drove Greg's Honda to visit Zion National Park, and stopped at Purgatory Jail on the way. I had a letter to drop off for Jeff. The receptionist told me he was getting out that day. I didn't know it was his day to be released. I wasn't sure I wanted to see him. I remembered him breaking my windshield.

The jail receptionist interrupted my thoughts. "Do you want me to tell your son that you are waiting to pick him up?"

"Don't tell him to expect a ride," I answered. I almost left, but instead I called Greg who was in California.

"It would be nice to see Jeff." Greg said.

I had come to Utah to breathe the fresh mountain air. Yet I was about to get something much better.

Jeff looked the best I'd seen him in a long time—clean and wearing boots and a cowboy shirt. We sat and talked for an hour in the jail lobby. He called a few sober houses. Then, while waiting for the sober houses to call him back, we drove to Kolob Canyon.

Our sixteen mile drive up Kolob Canyon was the most beautiful drive I've ever been on—through endless green grasses and pines. But the gas tank said Empty before we reached the end. I pulled over to ask a man if there was a gas station nearby. He replied, "No, but you should keep going to the end of the canyon because it's too beautiful to miss. You can coast out of the canyon if you run out of gas. I've coasted out of here with my truck's gas tank on empty several times."

We made it to the canyon's end—with its peaceful and still reservoir. Then we coasted back down the canyon. About that time, it got dark. We parked by the Virgin River to camp for the night. Jeff handed me a pack of cigarettes he'd had in his possession when he was arrested a few months earlier, saying, "Take these and do something to get rid of them." Then he walked down to the river.

With his pack of cigarettes in my pocket, I searched the terrain, found a hollowed-out tree trunk, mixed the cigarettes with sand, and buried them. Then I walked to the river and saw Jeff sitting by the bubbling waters, contentedly.

That night, Jeff snuggled in a blanket on the sand by the river. I handed him a flashlight and some papers I'd printed off the web about a two-year rehab called, Welcome Home.

Before falling asleep in the Honda, I looked out of my window and saw Jeff holding the flashlight up to the papers. He heard my movement in the car and shone his light my way. "Two years is a long time for a rehab," he said.

"It may be the best two years of your life," I replied.

I slept in peace that night, near my wonderfully sober son.

The next day we filled our gas tank next to a used bookstore. We went inside to look for books and once more resumed our hobby of reading.

Near St. George, we stopped at the home of Will—the man in the wheelchair who we'd taken in during a rough patch in his life. Will and his wife invited Jeff and me to spend the night and we fit right in. We explored their backyard canyon location, and enjoyed the feeling of love in their home. Then Jeff slept on their recliner and I slept on their couch.

We left Will's home the next morning so Jeff could check into a sober house. When we got there, they said they wouldn't be ready for Jeff until the next day. I slept in the Honda in a grocery store parking lot and offered to let Jeff sleep in the car too, but he declined and walked off to sleep in an alley. At 5 AM he returned, saying, "I'm walking to Labor Ready to register for employment before checking into the sober house." Then he said, "Cockroaches were crawling all over my head and face while I tried to sleep." He let out a laugh as if his ordeal was humorous. "When it cooled down," he added, "they went away."

Jeff liked making it on his own—getting a job and paying for his own food and clothes. He was happy when he worked. And he seemed to prefer being independent and sleeping with cockroaches over depending on others for support.

Jeff lived at the sober house for two weeks, but was kicked out for drinking from a vodka bottle in the middle of a recovery meeting. He continued working full time, though, starting at 5:00 every morning. He slept in a tent on the outskirts of town. I loved getting calls from him. He talked fast and slurred, but it was wonderful to hear that he was still working and happy.

One day he called to tell me that he'd been hired to help build a basement annex for the St. George Temple. He wanted to sober up for that. Jeff went to my Mom's house and asked to go to church with her, but she said, "No," because he didn't look well-groomed enough. I was mad that she turned him away, but anger does no good. Ron—a recovered addict—had told me that as a teenager he had been turned away from his first AA meeting because the people there told him, "You don't belong here. You're too young." He used drugs and alcohol for another twenty years before cleaning up. "In the end," Ron said, "It doesn't matter whether people accept you or not. What matters is that you want to be sober more than anything in the world."

Unlike Ron, Jeff didn't wait twenty years before attempting to go to church again. He bicycled to church the next Sunday, by himself. Yet when he surveyed the church parking lot, it was empty. "It was really strange to see the Church parking lot empty on a Sunday," he told me. He didn't know that church was held elsewhere for a conference in a larger building that day. "I'm proud of myself for staying out of jail," Jeff said. He sounded happy.

July 2013: Greg and I told Jeff we'd take him to Glacier National Park, Montana if he tested clean. Jeff looked forward to visiting his brothers who had summer jobs there. Unfortunately, Jeff failed the drug test and cried when we left for Montana without him. He kept calling us while we were driving, saying, "I want to see my little brother Matt."

In Glacier, Matt told us about when he watched the moon set and the sun rise at the same time, "A pink cloud encircled me on top of the mountain. There are no words to describe the amazing feeling I felt!"

Later, Matt took us backpacking. He taught us how to be safe if a Grizzly bear charges: *Avoid eye contact, stand your ground and get you pepper spray ready.* One grizzly charged the hikers in front of us but stopped mid stride, swung back and forth, and then to our relief walked away. We saw the last of the bear footprints trailing off on the other side of the river.

During our 12 mile hike to Cracker Lake, Matt's 11-year old niece who was hiking with us got tired. I told her before we left that I thought her 700 page book was too heavy for her backpack, but she underestimated the difficulty of the hike and was unable to keep up. I removed her treasured book, wrapped it in plastic, stuck it in a hollow tree, and said we could pick it up on our way back down the mountain. Tears began to fall from her eyes. Matt dried her tears and carried her book and her backpack too. Eventually Matt was also carrying my bedroll and going without water so I could have his when I ran out. I cherished his selfless love, saying, "You remind me of the young men in Wyoming who carried an entire company of freezing and emaciated pioneers across a wide river flowing with ice chunks. I heard that Brigham Young said, 'I don't care what weaknesses those boys had; their salvation is sure because of their sacrifice.' Whatever your faults are Matt, I hope you know God loves you, especially because of your love for others." Then I added, "If one of us passes on, a link of our family will be missing. Yet another family member will pass and they'll link together above. Then another, and another… until we are all linked together again."

I'd never seen Matthew as happy as he was while we were together, nor as sad as when we left.

Passing through St. George on our way back to California, Greg and I visited Jeff who was pretty drunk. We hugged him and said, "I love you," before he rode off on his bicycle.

"I wonder how Jeff has been able to stay alive," Greg said, without knowing at the time that we had already lost a son.

A few hours later, a ranger called us and said that Matt fell while hiking, and did not survive. Our family was devastated, especially Jeff. He drank himself into a stupor and ended up in Purgatory jail. The guard checked on him every fifteen minutes during his first few days there, to be sure he was still alive.

Jeff remained in jail for a month. Then Greg took him to Glacier National Park, where others of our family also gathered for a celebration of Matt's life. Jeff took a hike up the mountain where Matt had his accident. When Jeff returned, he said, "A butterfly landed on my shirt when I started my hike and didn't leave until I stopped to look at the view."

That night beside our cabin, horses and alpacas grazed as Jeff sat on the front porch stroking the fur of a stray dog. There was a glow in the sky from the moon.

At dawn, our family hiked to Avalanche Lake where a dozen waterfalls cascaded from thousand foot cliffs above. Jeff, Phil and James scrunched into a two-man inflatable boat and rowed across the water singing silly songs as sunlight sparkled all around. Later, a mother moose and her baby stepped into the water beside us. A little bear cub ran out of the woods and spun in circles at our feet as the sun went down.

Greg and I took Jeff home to California after Matt's Memorial. But the next day, Jeff went back to St. George.

He got a job at Labor Ready and called me frequently to tell me how he was doing. Snow filled up the canyons where he slept in his tent. Record-breaking low temperatures came. Jeff stopped calling home. Christmas came without me knowing whether Jeff was dead or alive.

CHAPTER TWENTY

One day in January 2014 I was talking to my neighbor in Simi Valley. "It was nice to see Jeff at Wal-Mart," she said. "He was panhandling, and I gave him a banana."

"What?!" I exclaimed. "You saw Jeff? He's in California?" I breathed a sigh of relief, *He's alive.* I drove to Wal-Mart to see him. He told me that in December he'd bought a bus ticket and rode to California with his pet rat in his pocket. He showed me his rat, which he named "Pocket." We had a nice visit, and he offered to share his food with me, without asking anything in return.

August 2014 Diary: I'm up in the night writing. I suspect Jeff is sleeping somewhere in Simi, but I don't know where. There's a slightly cool breeze. If Jeff is alive he's probably enjoying the stars and the comfortable temperature. Recently he was electrocuted by a policemen's Taser gun and tranquilized during an arrest. I don't mind him going to jail. When he does, he becomes his sober self again.

September 2, 2014 Diary: Jeff agreed to interview at Casa de Vida in exchange for the privilege of living at home for a week. At the end of the week we drove there. He received a warm welcome, and was accepted.

"I just came to interview. I'm not ready to stay here yet," he replied. Then he went to the hills. Like a child jumping into a river, he's oblivious to a strong current headed toward a dangerous waterfall.

September 3, 2014 Diary: I lie by our backyard pond where Jeff sat with me a few days ago. As I watch feathery clouds, I imagine Jeff can see them where he's at in the hills. I miss him.

Jeff came home, asking for the breath test, saying, "I tried to wait until the alcohol wore off before coming home."

Sometimes he pours cans of malt liquor from his backpack onto our flowers. Greg and I keep giving him graduating house privileges based on how long he stays sober.

October Diary: Jeff has been in the hospital's psychiatric ward three times in one month. He's been in jail for public intoxication over a hundred times.

Although he's intoxicated, and Greg and I make him sleep outside, he keeps coming back. I hug him and say, "I love you so much." I feel Matt brought him home.

November 11, 2014 Diary: I opened the window blinds and saw Jeff's bicycle parked under the juniper tree. The sight is like air to breathe for a drowning person. My son is home safe!

The last time I saw Jeff, he was standing in the rain in our driveway. He said he just wanted to say Hi. He wasn't ready to drug or alcohol test. I didn't want him to leave. "You can sleep in my van until morning," I told Jeff. But Jeff said he only dropped by to say Hi, and then he left.

December 2014: Jeff's visits warm my heart. We fed him outside where he slept under our juniper tree. With appreciation he said, "You're spoiling me!"

Later, we allowed him to sleep on the couch. Once more he fixed my van. He spent only ten dollars at the auto parts store to repair what the professionals couldn't fix for a thousand dollars.

Some people say we shouldn't let Jeff come home until he's gone to a rehab. But we're happy to see him. One never knows how short life may be, and how little time we may have together.

In 2015 and 2016 Greg and I served as missionaries in Historic Nauvoo—a Jamestown type of place in Illinois. There, Greg demonstrated how to make horseshoes, bricks, and Browning rifles while I baked bread in brick ovens. At night, we put on shows for tourists. It was the best time of our life. At first, while we were on our mission, Jeff couldn't stay out of jail. His phone calls from jail and the knowledge that he was safe and warm comforted me. It was during that time that a social security employee called me about Jeff being in jail.

"Could you put him on permanent jail status?" I asked, "He's a drug addict and getting government checks is a bad thing that puts his life in danger." The government employee stopped Jeff's disability and Greg and I paid his medical insurance and other legitimate needs. Eventually Jeff learned how to live his days outside of jail without getting arrested.

February 1, 2017 Diary: Jeff calls me on the pay phone at Wal-Mart every week. He panhandles for change to make the call. Even when he's drunk, he keeps calling to say, "I love you." The last time he called he was happy, laughing, and glad to say Hi!

Sandra called when she turned 40. "I'm not married, and I've always wanted children," she said with great sadness. My tears joined hers. Sandra said she's still praying for Jeff.

I went to the beach with my family and kept staring at the sailboats. A dozen of them floated in the sparkling water.

Nostalgia. *I picture myself looking up through the porthole, seeing the moon and the stars. I hope someday Jeff will get a sailboat and take me sailing.*

September 17, 2017: Greg and I attended a Twelve Step Meeting for help in the face of our difficulties with Jeff. On our way home we passed Jeff's Bridge—a place where we sometimes see him.

I remember the last time we saw Jeff by this bridge. He was splashing in a stream of water, like a child at play. When he saw us climbing down the rocks, his face lit up in an enormous smile. He stood to his full height, walked up on the rocks to greet us, and exclaimed in delight, "You came to see me!"

This time, when we approached the area, we saw a man climbing over a wall, headed toward the bridge. It looked like Jeff.

I was out of the car before Greg came to a complete stop, calling, "Hey Jeff! I'm so glad to see you!" Jeff turned around and came back over the wall. We exchanged hugs and said, "I love you." He didn't want anything—not even water. He said he was fine. We pass this way so seldom, but when we do, there he is.

In October 2017, Jeff dropped by our house. He had on bunny ears, a glittery headband, a pearl necklace, a nice T-shirt, a ragged jacket tied around his waist, and pajama bottoms that only came to his knees. And he had on shoes! Delighted, I hugged him and told him I loved him.

November 18, 2017: Jeff came home hungry and in pain, with bare feet and his hands wrapped in rags. Greg took him shopping. Then Jeff laid on the floor next to a bed in the garage where I was resting. He ate, played the harmonica, and talked a lot. I didn't realize at the time how drunk he was. I fell asleep while he and Christy were talking. Her compassion toward him touched my heart. Lately, she's been a recipient of Jeff's gifts that he brings home—like a beautiful bouquet of flowers he picked out of the florist's trash bin. Christy graciously smiled and thanked him, loving her brother even though he was drunk, wearing filthy clothes, and babbling.

Later, after Jeff left, Greg suggested we visit outside the next time he comes. He'd been drinking swigs of vodka beside me where I slept in the garage. I didn't argue with Greg. I also decided to put a sheet under him on his next visit, to catch the trash falling out of his pockets. I cleaned up Jeff's mess in the garage and found blood on the floor—his feet or hands had been bleeding. No wonder he moaned and cried while he laid there in rags, with no shoes, and his hands in bandages.

In January 2018, I met Linda, a woman who left her rich husband to go live with the homeless. She's my age and told me she invited Jeff to her camp to read Bible stories with her. "He was attentive and sweet," she said.

Another man I'd never seen before saw me looking for Jeff by a convenience store. He told me he knew Jeff. "Whenever I see him," the man said, "I buy him something to eat."

Another man, Rich Anderson, saw me at church and told me that whenever he sees Jeff he takes him to McDonald's to buy whatever he wants. Once, when Jeff ordered ten Egg McMuffins, Rich asked, "Are you going to eat them all?"

Jeff replied, "No, these are for the people in the camps."

I read in a book written by a 14-year-old Japanese boy that autistic people like to run away. It's an escape from their pain of having speech and body motions that don't come out right. They are aware of their difficulty fitting in with others.

Jeff finds peace, quiet, and serenity in the homeless camps. One might think there's a big crowd of homeless people living together. But really, there's not a lot of socializing. The camps are isolated one from another.

February 2018: I saw Jeff. He was wearing shoes, his hair was combed, he was clean shaven, and his clothes weren't torn. He continues to decline my invitations to come home. *What can I do to help Jeff?* I pray. God whispers, *Finish your book.*

April 26, 2018: Greg and I picked up Jeff from jail and brought him home. After eating and taking a bath, Jeff relaxed under our Juniper tree as we read together from Isaiah—a passage I never understood before: *It pleased God to see Christ suffer!*

It finally hit me—the real meaning: It didn't please God to see His Son suffer! No! Rather it pleased God to see Him get *through* it, to the other side. Because of autism and addiction, Jeff does not feel at home in this world. *Perhaps he pleases God, simply by getting through what he suffers.*

July, 26, 2018: I was about to go to bed when I felt prompted to wash my laundry. After doing so, I said to myself, *I'm so caught up on housework that if Jeff came home, I'd be able to give him my full attention.* Fifteen minutes later he knocked on the door. Sober.

His two bikes were stolen so he came home on foot, suffering a headache that made him cry. Greg gave him ibuprofen and I gave him the dinner Greg had fixed for me earlier—which I hadn't been hungry for. After Jeff ate, I gave him a head massage and he fell asleep.

July 27, 2018: Jeff's headache is so bad that he says he wants to be run over by a train, or see a doctor. I assumed his headache was from alcohol until I felt prompted to ask *why* his head hurt. Then, before I could ask, Greg asked *why* his head hurt.

Jeff replied, "It might be from when I got kicked in the head in jail a few hundred times, or when I fell asleep at a construction site and got kicked in the head."

July 28, 2018: Jeff is still with us. He even bathed. Time stands still. There's no stress around Jeff. Only peace.

He finally let us take him to Simi Valley's Urgent Care. After filling out paperwork and giving it to the receptionist, she said the doctor would not see him because it was time to close. Afterward, Jeff refused to go to the emergency room.

The next day Greg and I took Jeff to Los Angeles where we rent an apartment for a week every month while Greg serves in a temple. Greg left us resting in our apartment while he went inside the temple. I volunteered to help a neighbor get ready for a wedding brunch and Jeff came with me. Jeff is three times stronger than anyone I know, and never passes up a chance to help. Yet when he started to lift a table for my neighbor, he set it down, saying, "My head hurts too much for me to lift anything."

In alarm, I sent a message for Greg to leave the temple early. I talked Jeff into going to the emergency room at UCLA—one of the best hospitals in America, and only one mile away from our apartment.

At the emergency room Greg and I waited for Jeff to be seen. He said his pain was at a 3 (on a scale of 1-10). Yet he could hardly bear his headache. Greg and I repeatedly talked him into staying when he wanted to just leave. He cried softly.

Finally the doctors saw him. They were surprised at how quietly he presented himself when they found out what was wrong. He had a subdural hematoma, or bleeding on the brain. The layer of blood around his brain was a centimeter wide!

Within minutes they announced that they had a team of doctors waiting upstairs to perform emergency surgery. Jeff asked for a paper and pen. He wrote a note to the girl in the hills who delivers babies and who doesn't like Jeff to drink.

Dear Leta, I love you forever. -Jeff

Then he gave me his ring to give to her.

Two hours later, the accumulation of blood had been removed to release the pressure. His skull was sewed back together. A hole had been drilled through his skull to drain the residual bleeding through a tube coming out of the hole.

I walked to the hospital everyday. Walking healed my own pain. But one day when I was halfway to the hospital, I grew too tired to continue. At that moment, I met a young woman who offered me a ride. In her car she had food and clothes for the homeless. She was like an angel.

In the hospital, I got to know Jeff's nurse Nancy. After one of our visits, she said, "You and your husband are the most amazing couple I've met while working here."

I replied, "We're not as perfect as we seem. I went through 13 years of mental illness and still relapse when I'm tired!"

"We all pick up unhealthy things in life," she said. "We all have things to rise above."

August 1, 2018, UCLA Hospital Intensive Care Unit: The sunlight shines through Jeff's window onto his head. He's oblivious to the bright light, sleeping all day except for when the medical team awakes him to see if he remembers his name and can wiggle his toes.

Now the sunlight on his head flashes in a dazzling Kaleidoscope of light as the blades of an emergency helicopter whirl outside his window. Dark shadows fill the room as the body of the helicopter blocks the sun. As the helicopter moves higher, sunlight once more blinks and spins on Jeff's head. Finally, the helicopter leaves. A few days before coming here, Jeff and I were delighted to see helicopters fly past our balcony.

Watching Jeff sleep, I remember his premature birth.

There were oxygen tubes, monitors, and IVs hooked up to him. Around-the-clock nurses pricked his feet for blood tests. He screamed when the needle touched his skin!

Now, when the nurses ask for blood, he wiggles his hand out from under the bed covers and he sticks his finger out without even opening his eyes.

On August 5, 2018, Jeff was making a grilled cheese sandwich back at our Los Angeles apartment. Eli's wife messaged, "We had an earthquake in Bali while in the airport, waiting to fly to Australia. Half the planes are grounded but we are safe."

Greg started to make a nerdy joke, saying, "So the airplanes have half their wings?" Jeff jumped in with, "The plane will get them halfway to

Australia!" I laughed as Jeff served me the best grilled cheese sandwich I'd had since the last time he cooked for me.

Later, while resting, Jeff heard me make phone calls in search of a replacement window for our nearly thirty-year-old van. Two months earlier, while camping in Kentucky, Greg had slammed the back door and its big window shattered into thousands of pieces. After two months of making inquiries about replacing the window, we discovered one man who had one and said it would cost $750.

Jeff asked for my phone. He called the wreckers where he used to get used car parts. They replaced the window for only $75.

August 11, 2018, Diary: Greg and I arranged to stay a whole month at our Los Angeles apartment to be close to UCLA for Jeff's follow-up doctor's appointments. But Jeff left yesterday. Heartbroken, I found comfort in the temple.

August 15, 2018, 7 AM: I lie on the couch in our apartment where Jeff used to lie, my head hurting as if Jeff gave me his headache. I have dreams, disturbing dreams. *God hold me together so I can be there for Jeff.*

2:30 PM: Jeff called from Lancaster, a two hour drive from here. He said he took the wrong train to Simi Valley and ended up in Lancaster where he's spent a few days. He sounds terrific! I told him we'll pick him up at the train station and bring him back to our Los Angeles Apartment. I'm so happy!

The Next Day: Jeff's back. He was happy when we picked him up. The people at the train station seemed like angels. They loved Jeff and spoke to him with kindness. Jeff makes friends with people the way a puppy dog can wiggle its way into your heart. He was wearing a tail and holding the stuffed husky dog that I gave him in the hospital. Jeff also wore around his neck a colorful collection of trinkets tied on a string.

Jeff was a little drunk and we asked, "If we take you to Los Angeles, can you stay sober?"

"Sure. That will be no problem at the temple apartment," he replied.

We drove around Lancaster, looking at old cars—even an old Mercedes like the one Jeff had in his college days. Being with Jeff made the town of Lancaster appear romantic and exciting. Apparently, when he took the wrong train, he had no money to pay, they didn't ask for it, and he didn't know where he was going.

"I slept at the graveyard," Jeff said. "There were a lot of police at a building nearby. A few days earlier they had chased a guy there. He was running away from the police on top of a roof when he disappeared. Apparently, he fell in a crack between two buildings. They found his body while I was staying at the graveyard."

Now, at our apartment, Jeff's had a bath and looks better. No more crying in pain. He's healing.

August 20, 2018, Simi Valley: Jeff returned to the hills. Sometimes I think about heaven and it seems so near that I could almost walk into it. At times like this, I feel as if life is a miracle that never ends.

August 31, 2018: Jeff hung out with our family all day, talking with Tim and Brandy's family, Christy, Greg, and me. Tim's family had moved to the desert. Jeff made a point to be home when Tim came to visit. Jeff also talked to Butterfly on the phone until his homeless friends called. Then, when Tim's family went home, Jeff left.

Later, I heard Jeff's happy rap on the door while I was on the couch reading. I sprang to the door in delight! He was as sober as can be, although weary, and needing a shave, clean clothes, and a bath. He ate some Chinese food he had pulled out of a trash can which looked fresh and good, and he drank some apple juice I gave him. He'd been in jail for public intoxication. Now he sleeps on the floor in my room as I lie on the bed and write.

September: I prayed for Jeff not to drink too much and my prayer was answered. He came home 100% sober Wednesday night and stayed three days. He'd walked 2 days without shoes to get home. He told me he has a place to sleep every mile between the camps and our house—under a bush, in a ditch, or on a couch in an alley behind a store where the owner gave him permission to sleep. His only two open court cases are for sleeping on public property, and scavengering. When the people at Tico's Tacos Mexican Restaurant see him eat out of trash cans, they kindly offer him fresh food. *Angels. Angels are everywhere.*

Greg and I saw more of Jeff in August and September than we'd seen him in years.

CHAPTER TWENTY-ONE

In December 2018 Greg got a call from the hospital. Jeff had been run over by a car. His left leg was crushed so badly that a metal rod had to be inserted from his knee to his ankle, and one of his hands had been broken.

After Jeff had spent 9 days in the hospital, we brought him to our home to care for him in his recovery. We hoped he'd stay home forever. Patient and grateful, he amazed us by learning how to walk in spite of his pain. Yet—like with his other hand which had been broken years ago—Jeff didn't stay home long enough to keep his appointments to get the hand fixed. He hobbled through the woods with a sore leg and two broken hands.

Later, he was hospitalized for alcohol poisoning, and returned home to live with us again. It was then that he told me, "I feel bad for the driver who ran over my leg. It wasn't her fault. I laid down on the road with my sack of recycling cans because I was tired. I wish I could tell her to not feel bad about it."

Greg became Jeff's main caregiver, as I was not feeling well. Greg was patient, attentive, and calm. He continued to fast once a week in Jeff's behalf. If Greg's fasting days were added up back to back, they'd be four years of going without food.

Jeff left home. Yet he called to see how we were doing and to let us know he was okay. Greg's brother Doug said, "Maybe Jeff's meant to live in the hills. Maybe that's his mission in life."

Sandra called to say she'd like to move into our home to help care for me—and hopefully to be a friend to Jeff like she was in Utah.

Dear Jeff, I write this letter to you.
You can't read or hear the words I speak as I pen them down,
Yet I pray God sink my words into your heart.
Jeff I love you!
Thank you for being a part of our family.
You've blessed me, and many others.
You're adorable. You bring us happiness!
We miss you—more than Matt in a way—
For Matt's with God and is our guardian angel.
Yet you're on Earth—even within a hundred miles of my voice—
But I can't see you. I wish I could. -Mom

Mother's Day 2019: Phil's up to his elbows in mud cleaning out our old pond. He found some of Jeff's rocks including quartz, agate, petrified wood, and a rock with a tunnel through it. I lie outside where I can watch. My granddaughter Lexie calls the pond's fountain *a never-ending bubble.* A pleasant breeze picks up and birds sing. This is where Jeff and I often hang out in our yard. Hanging from the Juniper tree nearby is the sun Jeff gave me—which he pulled out of a trash dumpster. The circular sun is made out of 49 pieces of mirror—cut in rays like sunbeams. It dances in the breeze.

I just looked up and wished my mother a happy Mother's Day. She made it to 90 years of age before peacefully passing.

Jeff called to say *I love you, Happy Mother's Day.* He offered to help Sandra move to Simi.

Later, Greg drove me to Southern Utah to visit my mother's and Matt's graves, passing through the majestic red cliffs of Zion National Park. Sadly, Jeff wasn't around when we made the trip.

On our way back to California, we drove through Las Vegas and visited Sandra who has been delaying her move to our home.

Driving through downtown Las Vegas, I saw a homeless man who looked like Jeff—tall and gangly, with an innocent face and very messy hair. He even had a limp like Jeff. Greg took mercy on my cry of pity for the lost-looking man and pulled over.

I jumped out of the car and ran past the outdoor mall where I last saw the man walking. There were both well-dressed people and ragged homeless people on the sidewalk. The man was nowhere to be found—until I noticed the dirtiest bare feet I'd ever seen, sticking out from behind a huge power box that supplied electricity to the buildings.

I ran to the man laying there and gave him a whole, peeled, fresh pineapple which I had bought earlier. "Here's some food," I said. "You remind me of my son. What's your name?" He barely lifted his head and without making eye contact, said, "My name is God." I smiled and told him I was happy to meet him. Then I watched and saw "God" pick up the pineapple with unwashed hands and eat it lying down. He had juice running down his chin, neck and chest. I thought of Jeff. I hoped someone would show him the same kindness that I showed this stranger.

Later Jeff called from the hills from a borrowed phone and asked, "Did Sandra come yet?"

On June 13, 2019, I went with Greg to get our car serviced at a shop near the railroad tracks. I laid down on the grass near the tracks while waiting. It wasn't far from where Jeff lived with his 'family' by the tracks. Although they are homeless, they have beautiful surroundings: trees, flowers, fresh air, and nature. The trains going by are noisy, but except for that, the trains don't disturb anyone.

I called Claire, who has been my best girlfriend since Jeff was in diapers. We talked about Jeff. She said that when her sons struggled and she prayed for them, they'd end up in jail. That's what helped them sober up!

After our car was serviced, I felt depressed about going back home. I asked Greg to take me to the beach. I'd been getting 3 hours of sleep at night, and had nightmares. Years earlier, I'd read a book while on Santa

Rosa Island with Jeff which said nightmares are an opportunity to learn to be brave. We face danger in our dreams so we can be courageous in real life. I used my hours awake in the night to pray for strength.

I slept for a few hours in the car while Greg walked along the beach. Then, since the beach is close to the jail, I called to see if Jeff was there. The police officer said, "Yes, he was just picked up and he's still in the process of being booked. They might let him go today or tomorrow."

We waited for 8 hours for news about Jeff's status, but there was none. We wanted to know if they hospitalized him, or if they were holding him overnight, or keeping him for a while. We stayed overnight at a motel to be close to him.

On June 14, 2019 I went to the jail, awaiting Jeff's release. Lots of people were being let out. Some were well dressed, yet still staggering from drunkenness. Some were boisterous and loud. After all the others came out, Jeff walked out the door, happy to be free, but clearly not over the alcohol. We were glad to see each other, and I took him back to the hotel where he slept, crying out in his sleep. He later told me that his pain was from being kicked in his back when he was arrested. I hadn't wanted to go home to my housework. But now, after picking up Jeff, I found strength. Jeff gives me a reason to live when I'm tired—he takes me out of this world!

Back at home that night, Greg took care of Jeff, while I had a sleepover with my granddaughters in our backyard. They excitedly made private sleeping compartments out of blankets which they hung from the patio rafters! Their quarters were cozy with stuffed animals, night lights, fresh air and moonlight streaming onto their faces. I slept well and ended up staying on our patio couch for the next two nights, too tired to care for Jeff and our big house.

Jeff lied on the living room couch on a blanket, his smell permeating every room of the house. His hands and bare feet were black from dirt. Finally, he found strength to bathe. Then he came to a Hispanic Father's Day Dinner and Dance at the Church of Jesus with Greg and me and our granddaughters. He ate the Mexican food, relaxed, and then went back to the hills.

On June 16, 2019 Jeff, Phil, Christy, and Tim's family came over for Father's Day. I was too exhausted to get out of bed. My greatest joy came from seeing my grandson's make dinner at my bedside by cutting fruit and vegetables and stirring the salad and the deviled egg mixture. They picked oranges from our tree and made fresh juice.

After dinner, discouraged by troubled thoughts, I lay alone, sad.

Jeff, who had eaten our family dinner in silence, walked past my room and paused. "How are you doing?" he asked with concern.

I replied, "I have discouraging thoughts that I'm trying to get out of my head." Jeff's interest in my welfare touched my heart and uplifted me.

Diary, June 20, 2019: *Oh joy! Oh Universe, thank you! I'm with Greg and Jeff, resting in our yard. The juniper branches stretch out over our heads, as we recline in the summer breeze. Soft white blossoms bounce on a vine over our feet. The world is green, fresh and comforting. Jeff is in recovery. Greg cares for him, getting him food and water.*

June 22, 2019 Diary: I'm up in the night typing, overwhelmed. God tells me, *Relax.* I've been inspired to relax a hundred times in these last few days. *Why?* I suppose God has a plan and the answers are coming. I only need to go along with the flow. *Whoosh!* A feeling of validation comes, telling me that what I just wrote is truer than I know!

Jeff left our yard cluttered with clothes and dishes after his last visit. Greg just picked up the trash. Even though the whole house stank—before his bath—I'm just grateful to have seen him.

I tried to get Jeff to stay, but he left to visit his friends by the tracks.

June 26, 2019 Diary: I lie in the Pegasus Room of our home—a room named after a painting Butterfly painted on its door. Lovely, cool, fresh air comes in through the window. The Juniper tree outside has hundreds of miniature white pinecones on the tips of its branches.

Claire and I prayed for Jeff's return yesterday, and he returned. I'd been outside and when I came into the house, I found Jeff passed out drunk, but not so smelly because he had bathed last time he was home. I couldn't rouse him, so I prayed. God replied, *He can't be roused.* So I laid down on the floor beside him and read a book until midnight when he woke up. Then I helped him walk outside to his bed under the Juniper tree.

This morning he didn't remember that he had entered our house without knocking. He was surprised when I told him, and apologized. He was sad that he didn't remember. We read a scripture that says when we show kindness to others it's like showing kindness to God. "You've helped God a lot with all the things you've done for others," I told Jeff.

The juniper tree formed a lacey umbrella over us as we rested, allowing sunlight to dance on us through delicate boughs. *This fifty foot tree offers shelter, shade, and perches for birds. And this ole house holds lots of love.*

Jeff, Greg, and I shared meals and tender conversations. Then Jeff helped us transport a heaven-sent writing desk into the Pegasus Room. He said the broken bones in his hands had healed on their own. Later, Jeff left.

June 27, 2019: Jeff returned. We spent the day in Ventura together going to court and looking at boats. On the internet Jeff found a sailboat he wanted to buy.

June 28, 2019: Jeff left home, saying, "You can pick me up tonight by the cemetery." I missed a call from him while I was sleeping. Then I drove to the cemetery. I couldn't find him. It was dark and I didn't feel safe, so I came home and slept in my van in the driveway, surrounded by trees, stars, and the same fresh air that Jeff was breathing out there somewhere.

Seeing Jeff every few days means so much. Thank you God, I whispered. *You're welcome.*

June 29, 2019 Diary: A girl named Anna called me to say she was worried about Jeff. When I came to her camp, I liked her instantly—as if we'd known each other forever. However, Jeff was out of his mind with drunkenness. She handled him better than I could, so I invited her to join us in my van.

We took Jeff to look at the boat that he had found on the internet. When he saw the boat in the driveway he fell in love with it! In excitement, he stumbled out of the car and staggered up to the door of the house where the boat was. He was shirtless, barefoot, excited as a child, and swaying all over.

I called out, "No Jeff! Wait until you're sober to talk to the owner." But the next thing we knew, the owner came out, amused to see Jeff drunk and excited about his boat. Anna managed to get Jeff back in the van and apologized, saying "We'll come back later."

Then we stopped for hamburgers at Wendy's drive-in. Jeff stepped out of the van in the drive-through line and said Hi to strangers as if they were old friends he hadn't seen for a long time. Anna helped him get back in the van. Jeff minded her like an obedient child.

I invited Anna to stay the night. Jeff slept on his bed under the juniper tree and Anna slept on a cot nearby. During the night, I woke up repeatedly to the sound of Jeff's excited and loud voice. Anna quieted him each time, and I fell back asleep. I felt relieved to have Anna there, for I was too tired to check on Jeff.

June 30, 2019 Diary: This morning I visited Jeff and Anna by the Juniper tree. Anna seemed alright, but Jeff was more drunk than ever. He pulled out the biggest bottle of vodka I'd ever seen and drank from it in front of me. "Jeff, you can't drink here. This is where you come to sober up," I said. He tilted back his head and downed the remaining vodka before handing me the empty bottle.

"You're not allowed to drink on our property," I reminded him as I led him to my van to drive him back to the camps.

"I haven't had any alcohol," he said.

I wondered if the bottle had only water in it. Yet from the way Jeff swayed when he walked, he seemed pretty drunk.

As I drove toward the camps, Jeff let out a loud, mournful cry. It broke my heart. Amazingly, he managed to ask me a hundred times, "Are you going to look at the inside of that boat?"

I promised I would.

Anna walked toward her camp by the river. Jeff got out of my van too. Yet before he walked away, he stuck his head through the open passenger window, and said with a happy, determined voice, "Buy that boat! Buy that boat! Mom! Buy that boat!"

Then he walked away. I held my breath, hoping he wouldn't get in the way of traffic on the road, but he seemed to hold his course in spite of his swaying.

I moved my car to where I could watch him better while he walked off, my heart breaking. I prayed, confessing I couldn't help Jeff. I doubted his friends could help him either. I didn't even pray for angels like Matthew to help him. In desperation I prayed, *You're the only one God. No one can help him but you. I give him to your care.*

Tears ran down my cheeks. Then Jeff was gone.

Repeatedly, these words appeared in my diary: *I feel God's peace and guidance. I feel I must live without fear.*

Diary July 1, 2019, Dawn: Dear July, you are the month of my birth and the month of Matt's birth. What joy I have over being a parent! How can a mother not love her baby the way my mom loved me until the end of her life? That is the way I love my children!

10 AM: I took a walk and talked on the phone to Barb, the foster mom of some children in Kentucky that Greg and I have mentored.

Barb mentors me. She comforts me with her love and prayers for Jeff.

During our conversation, she stopped me. "I don't want to hurt your feelings," she said. "But have you ever thought that maybe you are trying to 'fix' Jeff, and maybe God has other plans for him?"

I'd never thought of that. I only knew that my plan was for Jeff to one day find sobriety and come home for good.

"We can't change anyone from the way they are," Barb said. "Only God can do that. We have to let go. Our plans are messed up. God's plans are the best! People are the way they are for a reason, and we usually don't know what that reason is."

We finished our call. Barb's words filled my thoughts.

Our plans are messed up. God's plans are the best.

At noon, I was sitting on the grass beside the Los Angeles temple, enjoying the cool, soft breeze while talking to Greg on the phone. He was at home, but planning to join me shortly. We were discussing our dreams and expectations for the future—and reminiscing Christmases when our children were small.

Abruptly, Greg interrupted me. "A policeman is walking to our door," he said, and he set the phone down.

Instinctively, I feared that something terrible had happened. I thought of Jeff and feared he was badly injured or dead. Why else would a policeman be walking up to our house? So I did the only thing I knew to do. I began to pray for strength to handle whatever the policeman said.

"Heavenly Father," I began. Instantly, God spoke, saying, *Remember, you gave him to Me. Whatever the policeman says is My Plan.*

Barb's words echoed: *God's plans are the best.*

My daughter Christy who was at home with Greg picked up the phone and told me that Jeff had been hit by a train. I cried there on the grass at the temple. He was dead. I remembered that I had given Jeff to God the day before.

The day which we fear as our last is but the birthday of eternity.
—Seneca

Death is not extinguishing the light;
It is putting out the lamp because the dawn has come.
—Rabindranath Tagore

CHAPTER TWENTY-TWO

I waited for Greg to come to our apartment in Los Angeles and lie down next to me and hold me. We needed to just hold each other and cry. Yet, we kept getting phone calls. While I waited for Greg, I pondered how much Jeff came home in the last few months—more than he had in years.

Memories drifted through my mind of Jeff as a little child. He would walk around the house with his cute little smile, saying, "Be happy. Be happy. Be happy."

Sometimes he'd laugh while sitting alone with no one else there. Just in his own private thoughts.

I'd like to think he's still saying, *Be happy.*

I called some of our children about what happened to Jeff—but I couldn't bring myself to call Butterfly. So I asked Tim to call her.

Butterfly later told me what happened when Tim called.

"The moment Tim called me it started raining. But the sun was still shining. It rained the whole time we talked on the phone. The gravel on my driveway sparkled in the sunshine. When we hung up, the rain stopped. Then a friend dropped by my house and asked why it was raining over my house, but nowhere else in town. It reminded me of when Jeff and I were young and we used to get excited talking about *Liquid Sunshine.*

I looked up songs called *Liquid Sunshine.* There was one with an awesome electric guitar—the kind that Jeff loved, by the Band *Liquid Sunshine,* with Sean Brobst, Doug Propst, Nick Buckley, and Fli Hoffman.

Walking down the only road, all alone and bitter cold
One thing, it'll probably be for life
And He says, *Buck up. Buck up*
The sun will shine upon you
But it's raining outside again
The overcast clouds everything I hold true
And he says, *Buck up. Buck up. The sun will shine upon you.*
—Lyrics by *Liquid Sunshine,*

That night, in his sleep, Phil said he felt a warm and wonderful hug from Jeff.

The next day, I was driving in unfamiliar territory. I actually missed the turnoff to Simi Valley and ended up at the beach. On my way home, I noticed that the oil was low in my van. Yet, I was too tired to pull over and search the web for a Jiffy Lube. Instead, I drove on, whispering, *Jeff, you're good with cars. Surely you can see the nearest Jiffy Lube from where you are. Please inspire me where to turn off.*

City after city disappeared behind me as I kept driving my van on the freeway. Then I had a feeling that I should take an exit. After exiting the freeway, I drove to the first shady spot I could see. It was a hot day. I parked under a tree and googled "Jiffy Lube" on my phone. To my relief, there was a Jiffy Lube around the corner.

Later, Greg told me about a tiny miracle he experienced. He said, "When the policeman was standing on our front porch, telling me what happened to Jeff, a butterfly flew up and fluttered between us.

These tender mercies lightened our grief.

At the funeral home, the funeral director Brittany told me that Jeff's face and upper body looked perfect. She was going to let me dress his body for the viewing.

The medical examiner, Armando Chavez said that Jeff's death was ruled an accident. "Many persons have been hit by trains," he said, "without realizing how fast the train is coming, or without hearing the train in time to get out of the way. Your son wasn't walking *on* the tracks, but off to the side. He was hit by the train's cow catcher—but it didn't pull him under—which is something I've never seen before."

I never asked Armando exactly what part of Jeff's body was hit. I like to suppose that it was only his leg. But for some reason it didn't matter.

Then, the day before Brittany and I planned to dress Jeff's body for the viewing, Brittany said to me, "I looked at Jeff's legs more closely and felt uncertain as to whether you'd still want to dress him."

At that moment, I sensed Jeff standing in the air above me telling me, *No.*

Jeff tried to protect me while he was alive.
He was still trying to protect me.

I replied to Brittany that she could dress him and thanked her for letting me know.

At the viewing, Jeff's hair was combed more handsomely than I had ever seen it. His large hands were folded on his chest over his red plaid shirt. As if asleep, he looked completely at rest, his face peaceful. I pictured a conduit of light from heaven vacuuming from our hearts our hurting memories and pouring in love and light.

My friend, Barbara Terry said, "Jeff was born in the wrong century. If he lived on a farm with all that energy, he would not only thrive, but he would have made the farm thrive too! He stayed with you until you were ready to let him go. Now God has better plans for Jeff in a place where the world can't hurt him anymore."

Tim shared a memory of Jeff collecting recycling cans. "Recycling is harder work than most people do in a day!" Tim said. "And once, when

Jeff's bags were full of cans, an older man came to collect where Jeff had just been. Jeff tossed his bags to the man and said, 'These are yours.'"

Tim suggested that Jeff began sacrificing his own needs for the benefit of others while in the womb. "Jeff must have let me take his air," Tim said, "because I was the one born with the healthy lungs."

Likewise, Phil said he remembered Jeff taking off his shoelaces and tossing them to a man with no laces. Then Phil added, "Not only was Jeff a giving person, but he was smart. He used to listen to lines people said on television. After hearing the lines only once, he'd repeat them back word for word.

Our Finnish foreign exchange student Toumas said, "I didn't hang out with Jeff much, but I remember when Jeff made me scrambled eggs. They were the best I ever had. When I told him, he just turned to me and started to laugh, saying, 'How hard can it be?'"

Jeff was buried beside Matt. Phil and Tim put 50 crimson red roses in a circle around their graves. My brother Steve got down on his hands and knees to smooth out the dirt and add more flowers.

Jeff's cousin had dug the grave in Orderville with a backhoe, and joined us for the service. A brilliant sunset and a quiet peaceful spirit enveloped us.

Earlier that day, Butterfly tucked a stuffed animal under Jeff's arm next to his pocket. It was an adorable gray and white rat. That made Tim think of the children's book: *If You Give a Mouse a Cookie.* So Tim put a cookie in Jeff's shirt pocket. He figured that if a mouse could start an adventure with a cookie, then a rat could too. Next, Phil tenderly placed flowers in Jeff's hands.

Before we left, Phil looked up, and said, "Goodbye."

CHAPTER TWENTY-THREE

At Jeff's Memorial Butterfly spoke. Here are her words:

Mom says, Jeff is a wonderful, caring, awesome, amazing person. If someone needs help, he will help them. He delivered babies. He went headfirst into raging fires. He carried the sick when they couldn't walk, he...

Uh... Wait a minute. Maybe we should just start from the beginning.

Jeff's journey through this crazy thing we call life started in this really cool "cave" that he shared with another fish like him who was always a bit too wiggly. One day the wiggly fish left the cave and it got really comfy in there. Jeff wanted to stay in his little cave a while longer, but just 8 minutes after the wiggly fish left, Jeff got pushed out into the big world too. He really wasn't ready and he almost didn't survive. Yet the doctors knew what he needed—they put him in a new cave. Jeff was happy just chillin' in his incubator. Who knew that the tiny little boy beneath that glass shell would turn into the giant of a man who was my big brother?

My brothers always had something fun going on in our backyard. They built a double-decker fort that was there for years. When we finally had to tear it down they dug a deep pit in the backyard and covered it with boards. This cave was a Super Secret Hideout. I have dreams that it's still out there and if you walk into my parents' backyard today you'd need to be careful to not fall into their underground cave system.

They also built go karts and had a track running around the yard. They would drive the go karts round and round for hours. Jeff loved to work on the go karts—learning to weld and fix motors. Jeff was always fixing things. The most memorable time that he fixed something for me was when he got a hold of my broken alarm clock. He took it apart and put it back together. We plugged it in, turned on the radio, and it worked! Then, seconds later, there was a big loud pop and the wall was on fire! The fire went out, and since we didn't actually burn the house down, we did the most logical thing we could think of. We took the alarm clock apart and tried to fix it again.

From a young age, Jeff had a paper route. I would wake up early when the stack of papers arrived at our house and help him fold them before he went on his route. Often I would ride my bike along with him. When I was big enough, I would run his route for him when he needed a day off, plus he'd give me some money.

He spent his money on lots of cool stuff—like fish. He had over a dozen fish tanks full of fish. He started breeding gouramis. They laid eggs, so we had to wait for the eggs to hatch. The Mollies had live births. We would sit in front of the tank for hours, watching the babies pop out of the Momma Molly until she wasn't fat anymore and the tank was a swarm of little bitty baby fish. We would name them as they came out. They had a lot of odd names that you never remembered for more than a second. Every time the Mommy fish would eat a baby before it fell beneath the protective mesh, we would say, "Oh no, she ate Bubble Butt," or whatever we decided that fish's name was at the moment. Jeff loved his fish. It was a fun hobby, and he was very good at it.

In 1994 an earthquake devastated his fish population. Every fish tank he owned, except one, was destroyed. The only tank that survived was the large one in the living room. The way the earth rolled, the couch bounced up against it and kept it from falling. We ran around picking up flopping fish from the ground, trying to save them. We put all our fish and the fish from the neighbors' broken fish tanks into that tank. Almost all of them died, so we cleaned up and repopulated our tank and had it for many more years. But it was never the same.

One day when Jeff was 10-years-old, Mom picked me up from kindergarten in our old blue VW Bus and we drove to Jeff's special school. I thought Jeff was amazing. He was so cool! To me his special school was not because he was slow. It was because he was so special that he got to go to his own school. On this day, I vividly remember him reading his spelling test. He spelled skeleton wrong. I blurted out, "I can spell it! S K E L E T O N. I was so proud of myself. This was the moment that I decided I was a genius. I could spell better than my awesome big brother. I never noticed the sadness he felt that his baby sister was spelling better than him. But he didn't get upset, he just sat there with me and let me read the rest of his spelling words.

Later in life, we talked about this incident on a day that he was struggling. I put my arm around him and he just started crying. He expressed how frustrating it is to be a full grown man, but not to be able to figure out the simplest things. He knew what he wanted to do, but just couldn't make it work the way it was supposed to. We all have moments when life is hard. We look at the task ahead of us and it's just Greek-Chinese soup. For Jeff, even ordering food at the drive-through could be confusing. He wasn't stupid, but he struggled—and the drugs didn't help at all.

Usually at funerals, you hear about how wonderful and amazing this person who died was, and by the time you walk away you are made to feel as if you've just buried a saint. In reality, they had their faults! We are all flawed in different ways. Some faults are avoidable. Some are not.

Mom said, *Jeff saved many lives and changed things forever for the better.*

Uh, wait a minute. I think we may have buried a saint—or possibly even a superhero.

But let's not get sidetracked.

Jeff loved rats and rodents. We had lots of them as pets when we were growing up. One day, our pet iguana fell into the rat cage. When we got home all that was left of our iguana was a piece of its tail. Those rats ate it all up. Jeff was mad. He liked the iguana a lot, so he wouldn't talk to the rats for over a week. I think the rats felt bad though 'cause when Jeff finally decided to talk to them again, they licked him like little puppies.

One time Jeff took one of my baby rats and put it in a cage with a mouse that lived in the garage with him. The rat grew up, and still got along with the little mouse. We really liked those two because they were an odd pair. One day they escaped. We always assumed they stayed together, though.

Later, there was a time when Jeff was arrested and had to go to jail, and he was very sad because he couldn't take his rat with him.

Now is the part where I talk about some of Jeff's flaws. As I began to write this, I kept feeling like I couldn't do it. I felt guilt that I was not there for Jeff. I always felt like, maybe if I would have done something differently I could have helped him. But I always remember that I tried. I used to say you can't help someone who doesn't want help. But what were we trying to help him do? Who were we wanting him to be? What expectations did we have?

Mom always had these fantastic dreams of turning Jeff into the person she wanted him to be. She would call me all the time and say "Oh, Jeff said this" or "Oh, Jeff wants to do that." I used to share these dreams, but about ten years ago I gave up. I didn't necessarily give up on Jeff, I just gave up thinking that Jeff should be the kind of person Mom wanted him to be.

I tried to get him to move to Kentucky, thinking it would be a great new life for him. He got out of jail and onto an airplane. He stayed with my family for a month, and though we had a lot of fun, it was just not going to work. All Jeff wanted to do was "Go home to the hills." That's when I asked myself, *What's happening? Who was I trying to make him be? What was I hoping for? That he'd get a boring job, live in a boring house and do all the things that regular people do?* He'd rather be living in the hills sleeping with the rats and rattlesnakes.

I chose a different life, one where Jeff didn't really fit in. It was hard to accept that we couldn't be as close as we wanted. I loved him and he loved me. But we both understood our place. He loved to see me when he was clean out of jail and when I was visiting California. I would go find him and say "Hi." Each year, though, Jeff's life got harder and more painful. In the past few years our visits turned to phone calls. Then most recently, I finally gave up on him being the kind of person that I thought he should be.

Jeff was a huge part of my life. I'd say the best years were from the time I was 16 until I was 21, when we worked together in a dog grooming shop. I spent almost every day with him. And if anyone knew us, you knew we worked hard. We were an awesome team!

One time, on our day off, we went to Lake Piru. We brought sun block, but didn't realize that we had left it in the car until we were already on the boat. We looked back at the shore and like idiots, said, "Aw, we don't need it anyways!"

We were badly sunburned by the end of the day. Jeff was the worst. He got blisters that oozed and bled. But Tuesday rolled around, and off to work we went. He brought extra shirts, so when he bled through one, he could change into another. It was horrible. But we always took care of each other.

Then I had my first child, Abby. My husband was deployed overseas, and I was a bit overwhelmed. I started making Jeff do more things for himself—small things, like keeping track of his own books at work. He struggled and he started using drugs again. I didn't like it, but I really didn't know what to do. So I let him do his thing. He'd been sleeping on my couch for a few years. Then I told him that when my husband got home from overseas he would have to start staying somewhere else.

As it neared the time when Dragonfly was to return home, Jeff started having a lot of problems. I went on a trip and Jeff worked without me for the first time. That was the day everything changed. They said he had a huge melt down, became violent, and then left. When I got back from my trip I didn't know where he was. Eventually he ended up in jail.

A year later, we tried to give Jeff another chance working with us at the dog grooming shop. I was excited, thinking that maybe I could get my Jeff back, but also nervous because there had been a lot of bad things happening over the last year—things that had really broken his spirit. When he showed up at work, I instantly knew we had made a mistake. He was behaving strangely and in less than an hour he was foaming at the mouth, with blood running from his nose. He started pacing, making growling, groaning noises. Then he started throwing dryers.

I went in the back of the shop and tried to talk to him, but he just started mumbling and I could tell he was angry. I didn't know what to do. I went to the front desk and called 911. I hung up the phone when I realized that he had followed me out. I didn't want him to know that I was calling the police. I'd always been the one to help him. I felt like I was betraying him. I didn't know what to do. He just stood there breathing heavy with this tortured look on his face, dripping mucus and blood. I was very pregnant with my second child, and I was scared. It was the first time in my life that I feared Jeff. The phone rang back since I had hung up on 911. The business owner Pam answered it and whispered that we needed help, hoping Jeff wouldn't hear.

When the police showed up he was mad! He walked right up to them, all 6 feet 7 inches of him, and started yelling at them. Four officers struggled with him, working to get him into cuffs. He was yelling, "Come on! Why are you ganging up on me? Why don't you take me one at a time?" Now, looking back I laugh, because there was Jeff, wanting to take the cops one on one, yet he was almost winning when it was four on one.

Jeff never wanted me to do drugs. In fact, he didn't like it when I drank. The only time I drank with Jeff, I got alcohol poisoning and hypothermia in the same night. I woke up covered in urine and vomit with an IV in my arm. Did you know going shot for shot with a 6 1/2 feet tall alcoholic is a bad idea? Apparently, I hadn't got the memo, so I made a Note to self, *Don't ever drink with Jeff.*

One of my Favorite Jeff Stories is when he needed a new flashlight. There was a store that had flashlights for $1, so he went there to pick one up. As soon as he set foot in the store, a worker started trailing him, watching his every move. Jeff was put off by this because he had been to this place many times and had never stolen anything. This man kept following him, watching him suspiciously. Jeff got to the flashlights and picked out the one he wanted, trying to ignore the man's glare. Then, as he passed the next aisle, he noticed an axe. He stopped, looked at the axe, looked back at the man, and then picked the axe up off the rack. He turned around with the axe in hand, looked the man in the eye, and dropped the flashlight into his pocket. Then he proceeded to the front of the store where he walked up to the register and paid for the axe. Jeff—the gruff 6 feet 7 inch tall man, with long dirty hair hanging in his face—slung his newly purchased axe over his shoulder and walked out the door. He had planned to spend $1, and instead spent $20 on an axe that he didn't even need.

Another one of my favorite stories is when Jeff was sleeping in a small cave that he dug in a hillside. There was a little snake that loved to come and share his warmth. He made friends with this snake, and sometimes he would carry it around in his pocket. After all, it wasn't the snake's fault that it was a rattlesnake. Here's the question I have wondered about, *If you were arrested, and the officer was bitten by your rattlesnake while searching your pocket, would that be considered assault with a deadly weapon?*

My big brother Jeff. He's the brother who wouldn't swim in a swimming pool, but would jump into an ice cold glacial lake. He'd put me on his shoulders and dance around until we'd get in trouble. He's the brother who'd sit on my house with a water hose protecting it from wildfires. He's the brother who carries me when I can't walk, and who stops me when I'm about to do something stupid.

Jeff has machete scars. Do you know anyone with machete scars? My brother had them on his arms and head. Do you know how he got them? From protecting somebody else!

You know, maybe he was a superhero. I've recently watched movies with my kids. Those superheroes have a lot of issues. Like every superhero, Jeff had his Kryptonite—the same kryptonite that ruined the lives of many people I know. His Kryptonite came in the form commonly referred to as Crystal Meth.

The story I'm sticking to is my brother Jeff is a Superhero armed with an axe and a flashlight.

Watch out for the rattlesnake in his pocket, and don't forget to say hi to his rat. I mean, he's got to have a sidekick, right?

So if you think your life's a big confusion
Because you never win the game
Just remember that it's a grand illusion
And deep inside we're all the same
-Lyrics from *The Grand Illusion,* a song by
one of Jeff's favorite bands, *Styx*

CHAPTER TWENTY-FOUR

Greg printed out 70 pages from his diary documenting his experiences with Jeff since his birth. I was deeply touched by what Greg wrote. Like me, Greg never gave up hope in Jeff. He wrote countless letters to Jeff in jail with encouragement, love, and tenderness. He traveled alone with Jeff when I wasn't there, took Jeff to doctors, and cared for Jeff's basic needs. When Jeff couldn't walk after brain surgery and being run over by a car, Greg was there.

At times I, as a mother, was more involved with Jeff than my husband. Yet from reading Greg's diary I learned things I never knew about Greg's activities with our children. For example, I never knew about the nightly scientific discussions he had with Jeff as a child, about whatever topic Jeff chose.

The last time that Greg was with Jeff, he bought him new clothes. He took a picture of how happy Jeff looked. He wrote in his diary, "With his lifestyle, I never know if it might be the last time I see him."

The last time I saw Jeff, he excitedly encouraged me to buy the boat we had looked at together. Within weeks, Greg purchased Jeff's boat, a 21-foot Hunter sailboat.

The first time we sailed it, Greg and I took Tim and his 8-year-old son Orion with us. The engine started having problems before we left the dock. It overheated. We hesitated to set sail without a working motor.

"I can't guarantee we won't have an accident," Tim said, "but I don't think there will be any loss of life."

Greg replied, "Let's sail."

The adventure began with Tim and Greg working the sails with their rusty skills. It had been nine years since they'd piloted a sailboat.

Within five minutes, we nearly ran into the rocks. Tim fiercely pulled the starter rope on the rusty motor and got the old thing smoking and coughing enough to save us from crashing. Then we turned the motor off before it could catch fire and headed out to sea.

The wind was gentle. Incredible peace wrapped around us. Tears fill my eyes just remembering that beautiful day. I sat on the bow with my feet dangling over the water, looking for dolphins. Tim and Orion stood beside me and then dove into the ocean for a refreshing swim.

With no motor, and only a gentle wind, we were so slow that kayakers out on the ocean pulled up alongside us to leisurely chat, before they passed us. The gentle rise and fall of the swells would have lulled me to sleep if it weren't for the ecstasy I felt in my heart. I knew Jeff was with us, especially when he played a trick on us.

The wind stopped. The sail dropped limp. The air was still. We sat motionless in the water for hours, with no breeze. I thought of the stories I've read about sailing ships in the 1700's. For days, passengers would be stranded at sea in stagnant waters.

I enjoyed Jeff's joke, relaxing on the calm and sparkling water. Yet when night drew near—and we had no phone reception at sea—I wondered, *What would Brandy think if her husband and oldest son didn't come home tonight?*

I started to pray for a breeze.

Ever so gently, the limp sails moved. A slight breeze put us in motion. Ships passed us while we moved at a snail's pace. Over an hour's time, our momentum picked up, and right before we reached the harbor we saw dolphins. Two of them simultaneously jumped out of the water. They were completely airborne.

Thinking back on the sight, I wonder if Matt and Jeff were cheering us on by coaxing those dolphins to jump high in the air. I've been looking for things to be thankful for ever since. A bite to eat. A chance to pray. A bird song. Sustaining love in my heart.

Like a candle in a dark tunnel, is love.

Words to a song by "Styx," one of Jeff's favorite bands:

Come Sail Away

I'm sailing away, set an open course for the virgin sea
I've got to be free, free to face the life that's ahead of me
On board, I'm the captain, so climb aboard
We'll search for tomorrow on every shore
And I'll try, oh Lord, I'll try to carry on

I look to the sea, reflections in the waves spark my memory
Some happy, some sad
I think of childhood friends and the dreams we had
We live happily forever, so the story goes
But somehow we missed out on that pot of gold
But we'll try best that we can to carry on

A gathering of angels appeared above my head
They sang to me this song of hope, and this is what they said
They said come sail away, come sail away
Come sail away with me...

I thought that they were angels, but to my surprise
We climbed aboard their starship, we headed for the skies
Singing come sail away, come sail away
Come sail away with me
Come sail away, come sail away
Come sail...

ACKNOWLEDGEMENTS

My heart overflows with thanks to those who helped me write this book. First, to Jeff for living the life he lived and sharing it with me. Second to Danielle Wheeler and Karrilynn Zoller for cornering me in 2010 and telling me I must write a book about Jeff. Third, to my husband Greg, my daughter Christy, Amy Stevenson, Tom Saulnier, Joy Lanctot, Irene Durham, Liz Tsukashima, Trisha Mills, and Barbara Terry for their editing assistance. Fourth, to the persons at Bookwhip who have most patiently helped me—each is a gem and an inspiration. Last but not least, I'm thankful to all of my family, my friends, and God for walking with me through this story.

Books Referenced

"The Reason I Jump," By Naoki Higashida

"Building the Bonds of Attachment—Awakening Love in Deeply Troubled Children," By Phil A. Hughes

"The Cay," By Theodore Taylor

"Heart-to-Heart Talk: A Clients Guide to Transformation in Psychotherapy," By Julia M. Landis

"If You Give a Mouse a Cookie," By Laura Numeroff

About the Author

Beverly Ann Needham has jumped over rattlesnakes, fought off wild dogs, shared her picnic blanket with a skunk, run marathons, slept with the homeless, raised 7 children with her rocket scientist husband, and been the "American Mom" to dozens of foreign exchange students. A former teacher, Beverly shares her heart-rending experiences with frankness and humility—to offer hope to those who are struggling.

Royalties I pray shall go
To help the poor and weary,
Revive lost dreams, restore dead hopes,
Where prospects may seem dreary.
B. A. N.

My family has recorded a few songs which may be found on Youtube under "Beverly Ann Needham."

dreamsrevived.org

CPSIA information can be obtained
at www.ICGtesting.com
Printed in the USA
LVHW111756181120
672046LV00052B/1486

9 781950 596911